Index to

Davidson County, Tennessee

Wills and Administrations

1784 to 1861

Will Books 1 to 19

Byron Sistler and Barbara Sistler

Janaway Publishing, Inc.

Reprinted by

Janaway Publishing, Inc.
2412 Nicklaus Dr.
Santa Maria, California 93455
(805) 925-1038
www.JanawayPublishing.com

2007, 2013

ISBN 13: 978-1-59641-099-2

Made in the United States of America

DAVIDSON COUNTY. TN WILLS AND ADMINISTRATIONS TO 1861: AN INDEX

This index covers all will books from 1784 through 1861--Books 1 to 18 and part of Book 19. The entries are relatively self-explanatory, but a few observations are in order:

The year shown is, where possible, year of the probate. Otherwise year of the will, or first year mention is found of the estate.

At the end of each entry is identification where the instrument can be found--wb (will book) followed by book # and page number. For example, wb-18-431 means will book 18, page 431.

In general, we attempted to insert notation regarding an estate only once, when it first appeared in the records. Exceptions were (1) if there was an actual will, the page number was shown even if there was a previous entry for that estate; (2) if a later insertion had been found with a more complete name--name instead of initials, etc.-- or a substantially different spelling of what seemed to be the same name; (3) if 10 years or more had passed since last entry for that name (it might be a different person with the same name).

Guardian proceedings and settlements are to be found sprinkled throughout the books. While these contain much data of genealogical value, we omitted these references as not within the scope of this particular work.

Where a single will book had two series of pagination--starting over with page 1 somewhere in the middle--we have marked the second set of page numbers with an asterisk.

Microfilmed copies of the original books are to be found (on eight rolls) at the Tennessee State Library and Archives in Nashville. In addition, a two volume set, *Davidson County Tennessee Wills and Inventories,* by Helen C. and Timothy Marsh is at the printer as this introduction is being written. It abstracts the records in these books from 1784 to 1832.

Byron Sistler
Barbara Sistler

Nashville, TN
July 1989

Abernathy, Laban 1833 wb-10-183
Abston, Joshua 1812 wb-4-197
Acord, Jonas 1851 wb-15-153
Adams, Andrew E. 1803 wb-2-331
Adams, Benjamin 1806 wb-3-134
Adams, David 1830 wb-9-368
Adams, Martha 1854 wb-16-310
Adams, Mary Ann 1853 wb-15-547
Adams, Richard K. 1818 wb-7-289
Adams, Thomas 1799 wb-2-160
Adams, William 1808 wb-3-197
Adams, William 1848 wb-14-173
Adams, Williamson 1822 wb-8-107
Adkisson, William J. 1857 wb-17-259
Alderson, Thomas 1858 wb-17-442
Alexander, Henry 1806 wb-3-118
Alexander, Thomas 1855 wb-16-536
Alford, George W. 1835 wb-10-401
Alford, John 1838 wb-11-189
Allcorn, Prudence 1854 wb-16-414
Allen, Alethia B. 1854 wb-16-453
Allen, Benjamin 1846 wb-13-412
Allen, Carter 1847 wb-14-97
Allen, Dixon 1835 wb-10-487
Allen, Dixon 1851 wb-15-27
Allen, George S. 1853 wb-16-204
Allen, Henry 1841 wb-12-153*
Allen, Isaac 1848 wb-14-234
Allen, Jane 1830 wb-9-461
Allen, Jeremiah 1823 wb-8-252
Allen, Jeremiah 1825 wb-8-419
Allen, John 1816 wb-4-429
Allen, John 1850 wb-14-472
Allen, Mathew 1837 wb-11-27
Allen, Richard 1850 wb-14-472
Allen, Robert 1815 wb-4-338
Allen, Robert 1815 wb-4-353
Allen, Thomas J. 1842 wb-12-324*
Allen, William 1831 wb-9-519
Alley, Elizabeth 1861 wb-18-431
Allford, Jane 1843 wb-13-3
Allison, Andrew 1861 wb-18-467
Allison, Hugh 1836 wb-10-548
Allison, Richard Harrison 1838 wb-11-172
Almond, John V. 1833 wb-10-205
Ament, Henry 1851 wb-15-75
Anderson, Elizabeth 1847 wb-14-115
Anderson, George 1854 wb-16-437
Anderson, George A. 1859 wb-18-313
Anderson, Jane 1846 wb-13-473
Anderson, Jasper 1837 wb-11-74
Anderson, John 1818 wb-7-288
Anderson, John 1837 wb-11-21
Anderson, N. S. 1851 wb-14-661
Anderson, Thomas J. 1855 wb-16-538

Anderson, William 1851 wb-15-17
Anderson, William P. jr. 1828 wb-9-272
Anthony, Philip sr. 1860 wb-18-218
Apple, George 1851 wb-15-183
Appleton, James 1840 wb-12-70*
Armstrong, Abner 1855 wb-16-487
Armstrong, Francis W. 1843 wb-12-447*
Armstrong, John C. 1851 wb-15-138
Armstrong, Martin W. B. 1827 wb-9-112
Armstrong, Robert 1851 wb-15-57
Armstrong, Thomas 1858 wb-17-485
Arrington, Miles B. 1853 wb-15-539
Arthur, Ann 1852 wb-15-461
Ashley, Nathaniel 1828 wb-9-162
Atherly, Johnathan 1808 wb-3-198
Athey, Thomas J. 1829 wb-9-343
Atkerson, Selah 1817 wb-7-125
Atkison, Celia 1816 wb-7-100
Atkisson, Miles W. 1860 wb-18-132
Austin, Edwin 1847 wb-14-101
Austin, John 1840 wb-12-14
Austin, John 1840 wb-12-75*
Austin, Patrick 1850 wb-14-550
Austin, Sarah Emily 1851 wb-14-608
Avery, John 1847 wb-14-41
Backus, George 1832 wb-9-577
Bailey, Robert 1830 wb-9-424
Bailey, Sterling A. 1815 wb-4-378
Baird, John 1825 wb-8-407
Baird, John W. 1819 wb-7-327
Baker, Charles 1796 wb-2-47
Baker, Francis B. 1844 wd-13-24
Baker, Hiram 1842 wb-12-310*
Baker, Hiram 1842 wb-12-320*
Baker, J. K. 1851 wb-15-206
Baker, John 1825 wb-8-456
Baker, John 1842 wb-12-275*
Baker, Judy 1854 wb-16-405
Baker, Nicholas 1792 wb-1-246
Baker, Williamson 1823 wb-8-274
Baker, Zach. 1803 wb-2-333
Baker, Zacheus 1813 wb-4-206
Balch, Alfred 1853 wb-16-182
Balden, Lenas 1809 wb-4-56
Baldridge, John L. 1834 wb-10-280
Baldridge, John L. 1834 wb-10-305
Ballew, William P. 1843 wb-12-460*
Ballow, Battenby 1828 wb-9-180
Balthrop, Henry F. 1855 wb-16-580
Bandy, R. C. 1861 wb-18-469
Bandy, Wilshire 1853 wb-15-481
Banister, Marshall 1845 wb-13-152
Banks, Samuel M. 1861 wb-18-612
Banzer, George 1851 wb-15-73
Barclift, Samuel 1848 wd-14-226

Barham, Elizabeth 1847 wb-14-33
Barham, Newsom 1840 wb-12-43*
Barker, William H. 1838 wb-11-404
Barkley, John 1806 wb-3-72
Barnes, Benjamin 1859 wb-18-92
Barnes, Henry 1832 wb-10-34
Barnes, Henry 1848 wb-14-249
Barnes, James 1841 wb-12-245*
Barnes, Jesse 1845 wb-13-243
Barnes, Jesse 1845 wb-13-295
Barnes, John M. 1852 wb-15-277
Barnett, Henry 1825 wb-8-444
Barns, Benjamin 1809 wb-4-75
Barrons, Elizabeth 1847 wb-14-33
Barrow, Ann E. 1831 wb-9-556
Barrow, Matthew 1856 wb-17-53
Barrow, Micajah 1806 wb-3-78
Barrow, Willie 1825 wb-8-483
Barry, Richard 1839 wb-11-584
Basey, Sims M. 1844 wb-13-61
Bashaw, Benjamin 1837 wb-11-80
Bass, Peter 1831 wb-9-465
Basye, Isaac 1814 wb-4-302
Bateman, Henry 1851 wb-15-9
Bateman, Isaac Newton 1848 wb-14-276
Battle, Isaac 1816 wb-7-53
Battle, William M. 1851 wb-14-659
Baugh, William 1800 wb-2-165
Bauhman, Jno. C. 1809 wb-4-36
Bayse, L. M. 1840 wb-12-138*
Beach, James 1851 wb-15-62
Bean, Daniel M. 1818 wb-7-270
Beasley, Charles 1816 wb-7-17
Beaty, David 1817 wb-7-142
Beaty, William 1815 wb-4-365
Beazley, John 1845 wb-13-181
Beazley, Sally 1847 wb-14-23
Beck, John 1808 wb-3-206
Beck, John 1814 wb-4-288
Beck, John E. 1818 wb-7-271
Becton, John Slade 1803 wb-2-307
Beeton, Asa 1809 wb-4-66
Beeton, Dorcas 1809 wb-4-66
Beeton, George 1809 wb-4-66
Bell, Benjamin 1848 wb-14-238
Bell, Clement L. 1834 wb-10-383
Bell, Daniel 1816 wb-7-10
Bell, Evaline 1861 wb-18-582
Bell, George 1822 wb-8-127
Bell, George 1830 wb-9-364
Bell, Henry 1816 wb-7-99
Bell, Hugh F. 1832 wb-10-12
Bell, Jain 1823 wb-8-251
Bell, John 1797 wb-2-73
Bell, John 1855 wb-16-465

Bell, Joseph M. 1858 wb-17-441
Bell, L. M. 1861 wb-18-466
Bell, Montgomery 1855 wb-16-589
Bell, Rebecah 1816 wb-4-476
Bell, Rebecca 1816 wb-7-79
Bell, Robert 1816 wb-4-447
Bell, Robert 1816 wb-7-77
Bell, Samuel 1821 wb-7-492
Bell, Samuel 1837 wb-11-82
Bell, Tabitha 1859 wb-17-624
Bell, Thomas 1839 wb-12-34*
Bell, William R. 1828 wb-9-189
Bennett, Henry 1824 wb-8-389
Benoit, Earnest 1832 wb-9-601
Benson, Isaac C. 1854 wb-16-327
Berkley, Rufus K. 1855 wb-16-486
Berry, Adam H. 1835 wb-10-527
Berry, Daniel 1852 wb-15-362
Berry, Keziah 1802 wb-2-258
Berry, Martha 1814 wb-4-319
Berry, Mary 1860 wb-18-192
Berry, William 1789 wb-1-122
Berryhill, Wm. M. 1837 wb-11-77
Beshaw, Benjamin 1835 wb-10-530
Bess, John 1851 wb-14-648
Best, John 1851 wb-15-191
Betts, Caty 1838 wb-11-121
Betts, Thomas 1845 wb-13-244
Betts, Zacheriah 1823 wb-8-218
Bibb, Benjamin 1826 wb-9-57
Bibb, Cary 1809 wb-4-28
Bibb, James 1809 wb-4-73
Bibb, James 1816 wb-7-67
Bibby, William 1842 wb-12-292*
Bibby, William 1842 wb-12-312*
Bigelow, Luther 1832 wb-10-30
Biggs, Reuben P. 1825 wb-8-486
Billew, Rebeccah 1803 wb-2-335
Binkley, Daniel 1825 wb-8-460
Binkley, Frederick 1858 wb-17-473
Binkley, John 1843 wb-13-2
Binkley, John H. 1849 wb-14-417
Binkley, Joseph 1840 wb-12-59*
Binkley, Robert F. 1860 wb-18-296
Bird, Richard 1808 wb-3-193
Birdwell, George 1816 wb-7-108
Bishop, Benjamin 1807 wb-3-160
Bittle, George 1860 wb-18-347
Black, John 1846 wb-13-469
Black, William 1843 wb-12-439*
Blackamon, Jno. 1787 wb-1-54
Blackamore, John 1803 wb-2-325
Blackfarr, William 1812 wb-4-177
Blackman, Charles H. 1861 wb-18-453
Blackman, Edmond 1816 wb-4-438

Blackmon, Edmond 1816 wb-7-20
Blain, John 1816 wb-7-17
Blain, John 1830 wb-9-450
Blair, John C. 1845 wb-13-246
Blair, William 1857 wb-17-292
Blair, William K. 1853 wb-15-510
Bland, Naoma 1851 wb-14-607
Bland, Naomy 1851 wb-14-601
Bland, Samuel 1833 wb-10-265
Bledsoe, George Ann 1849 wb-14-431
Bledsoe, Jesse 1840 wb-12-66*
Bledsoe, Willis 1847 wb-14-42
Bley, Philip 1818 wb-7-272
Blount, Reading 1831 wb-9-501
Blount, Thomas 1815 wb-4-348
Blount, Thomas 1832 wb-9-588
Boardman, William Z. 1856 wb-17-56
Boaz, Thomas 1834 wb-10-284
Bodine, J. M. 1837 wb-11-59
Bodine, John M. 1838 wb-11-480
Bonds, John 1833 wb-10-94
Bondurant, Edward 1821 wb-8-29
Bondurant, Jacob M. 1859 wb-18-85
Booth, Henry sr. 1813 wb-4-238
Booth, Peter 1826 wb-9-62
Boren, John 1800 wb-2-166
Bosley, Beal 1860 wb-18-327
Bosley, John 1844 wb-13-74
Bosley, Rebeccah 1788 wb-1-51
Bostick, Don F. 1839 wb-12-7*
Bostick, Harden P. 1861 wb-18-529
Bosworth, William 1859 wb-18-61
Botts, Jane T. 1842 wb-12-310*
Bowen, George T. 1829 wb-9-279
Bowen, Thomas 1804 wb-2-354
Bowers, Elizabeth Ann 1805 wb-3-116
Bowers, John 1803 wb-2-306
Bowers, William P. 1823 wb-8-247
Bowers, William P. 1841 wb-12-225*
Bowers, William P. 1852 wb-15-225
Bowle, John 1821 wb-8-31
Bowman, Samuel D. 1843 wb-12-412*
Bowman, Samuel D. 1843 wb-12-432*
Bowyer, John 1820 wb-7-452
Bowyer, Peter G. 1823 wb-8-167
Boyd, Andrew 1825 wb-8-409
Boyd, Elizabeth 1853 wb-16-130
Boyd, Elizabeth 1861 wb-19-24
Boyd, Elizabeth J. 1856 wb-17-64
Boyd, George W. 1830 wb-9-412
Boyd, James 1828 wb-9-215
Boyd, John 1838 wb-11-275
Boyd, John 1838 wb-11-426
Boyd, John 1853 wb-16-72
Boyd, Joseph B. 1846 wb-13-378

Boyd, Lamira 1838 wb-11-429
Boyd, Mary J. 1857 wb-17-228
Boyd, Nancy 1859 wb-17-610
Boyd, R. 1851 wb-14-674
Boyd, R. P. 1839 wb-11-537
Boyd, Racheal 1837 wb-11-43
Boyd, Richard 1825 wb-8-494
Boyd, Robert 1793 wb-1-300
Boyd, Robert 1853 wb-16-55
Boyd, Whitmell H. 1830 wb-9-390
Bradford, Elizabeth 1838 wb-11-291
Bradford, Elizabeth 1841 wb-12-120*
Bradford, John 1827 wb-9-122
Bradford, John 1837 wb-11-284
Bradford, Mary Jane 1835 wb-10-515
Bradford, Mary M. 1842 wb-12-301*
Bradford, Mary M. 1842 wb-12-318*
Bradford, Robert 1840 wb-12-84*
Bradshaw, John C. 1833 wb-10-213
Bradshaw, Joseph 1851 wb-14-661
Branch, Benjamin 1819 wb-7-352
Branch, Nancy 1845 wb-13-304
Brannon, James 1816 wb-7-52
Bransford, John 1838 wb-11-422
Bransford, L. M. 1857 wb-17-182
Bransford, Murray L. 1856 wb-17-149
Bransford, Samuel W. 1848 wb-14-258
Breathett, Edward 1838 wb-11-430
Breathitt, Edward 1837 wb-11-170
Brent, Elizabeth 1849 wb-14-430
Brent, Hugh 1825 wb-8-430
Brewer, Elisha 1823 wb-8-280
Brice, John 1827 wb-9-80
Brien, Emily J. 1860 wb-18-193
Briggs, Amos 1859 wb-17-576
Briles, Sarah 1855 wb-16-572
Briles, Sarah Ann 1844 wd-13-18
Brim, Daniel 1830 wb-9-460
Brinkley, Alexander 1823 wb-8-202
Brinkley, Eli 1857 wb-17-255
Brinkley, James 1855 wb-16-512
Brinkly, Alexander 1825 wb-8-410
Britain, Jno. S. 1860 wb-18-405
Bromaker, F. 1838 wb-11-288
Brooks, Christopher 1854 wb-16-394
Brooks, John sr. 1831 wb-9-472
Brooks, Matthew 1812 wb-4-182
Brooks, Moses T. 1861 wb-18-605
Brookshire, Fairley 1824 wb-8-294
Brown, A. C. 1841 wb-12-26
Brown, Aaron V. 1860 wb-18-134
Brown, Bedford 1826 wb-8-521
Brown, Daniel 1829 wb-9-348
Brown, Ezekiel 1817 wb-7-168
Brown, George 1851 wb-14-609

Brown, J. P. 1859 wb-17-604
Brown, J. P. W. 1851 wb-15-142
Brown, J. Z. W. 1851 wb-15-11
Brown, James 1795 wb-2-34
Brown, Jane B. 1847 wb-14-18
Brown, Jesse 1842 wb-12-258*
Brown, John 1795 wb-2-28
Brown, John 1836 wb-10-645
Brown, John D. 1843 wb-12-467*
Brown, John L. 1842 wb-12-258*
Brown, John P. W. 1852 wb-15-223
Brown, Josiah G. 1861 wb-18-469
Brown, Martha 1861 wb-18-569
Brown, Morgan 1840 wb-12-74*
Brown, Morgan W. 1853 wb-16-167
Brown, Moses 1838 wb-11-209
Brown, Moses 1838 wb-11-261
Brown, N. T. P. 1851 wb-15-3
Brown, Samuel D. 1853 wb-16-100
Brown, Thomas 1793 wb-1-282
Brown, Thomas S. 1818 wb-7-282
Brown, William D. 1859 wb-17-578
Brown, William H. 1828 wb-9-153
Brown, William L. 1830 wb-9-406
Brown, William P. 1841 wb-12-151*
Bryan, Hardy W. 1856 wb-17-146
Bryan, Henry 1853 wb-15-514
Bryan, Henry M. 1851 wb-15-139
Bryan, John M. 1857 wb-17-397
Bryan, Margaret 1841 wb-12-222*
Bryan, Mary 1858 wb-17-451
Bryan, Samuel 1832 wb-9-575
Bryant, James 1798 wb-2-128
Bryant, James 1838 wb-11-326
Bryant, John 1857 wb-17-302
Bryant, S. B. R. 1860 wb-18-281
Bryant, Sarah 1857 wb-17-385
Bryant, Sherrod 1854 wb-16-431
Bryant, Sherwood 1855 wb-16-583
Bucchanan, Samuel 1793 wb-1-293
Buchanan, Archibald 1851 wb-14-675
Buchanan, James 1851 wb-15-13
Buchanan, Jno. 1787 wb-1-69
Buchanan, John 1833 wb-10-133
Buchanan, John K. 1861 wb-19-26
Buchanon, Alexander 1838 wb-11-113
Buchanon, Alexander 1838 wb-11-155
Buchanon, Archibald 1806 wb-3-120
Buchanon, James 1841 wb-12-152*
Buchanon, Robert 1829 wb-9-332
Buchanon, Robert 1841 wb-12-212*
Buchanon, Samuel 1817 wb-7-133
Buckanan, Samuel 1813 wb-4-241
Buie, Daniel 1837 wb-11-107
Buie, David 1829 wb-9-281

Buie, David 1839 wb-11-579
Bullock, Charles 1815 wb-4-382
Bumpass, John G. 1855 wb-16-461
Burge, Thomas C. 1861 wb-18-505
Burgess, Priscilla 1859 wb-17-580
Burke, Carter 1849 wb-14-425
Burkley, Rufus K. 1860 wb-18-232
Burleigh, Elizabeth 1860 wb-18-400
Burnett, E. H. 1859 wb-18-90
Burnett, Henry 1817 wb-7-213
Burnett, Henry 1827 wb-9-116
Burnett, Jeremiah 1840 wb-12-23*
Burnett, Leonard 1852 wb-15-312
Burnett, Peter 1854 wb-16-438
Burnett, Polly 1806 wb-3-127
Burnett, Rebecah 1806 wb-3-127
Burnett, S. H. 1852 wb-15-378
Burnett, Sally 1806 wb-3-127
Burnett, Samuel H. 1854 wb-16-374
Burnham, Newton E. 1826 wb-9-28
Burnsides, Thomas 1807 wb-3-175
Burrows, Charles 1816 wb-7-6
Burton, Ann 1845 wb-13-194
Burton, C. P. 1857 wb-17-380
Burton, George H. 1846 wb-14-2
Burton, Samuel C. 1843 wb-12-390*
Bush, Carter 1847 wb-14-33
Butler, A. W. 1854 wb-16-359
Butler, E. C.. 1854 wb-16-328
Butler, Edward 1854 wb-16-294
Butler, John R. 1855 wb-16-594
Butler, Micha 1856 wb-16-616
Butt, Samuel 1851 wb-14-589
Byers, Susannah 1858 wb-17-519
Byres, David P. 1845 wb-13-177
Byrn, James 1825 wb-8-450
Byrn, William P. 1829 wb-9-306
Bysor, Mary 1851 wb-14-589
Bysor, Peter 1832 wb-9-611
Cabler, B. G. 1854 wb-16-357
Cabler, Fredrick 1841 wb-12-260*
Cage, William G. 1848 wb-14-281
Cage, William G. 1849 wb-14-415
Cagle, Charles 1823 wb-8-209
Cahal, Ann C. 1856 wb-17-110
Cahal, Terry H. 1852 wb-15-253
Calcote, James L. 1860 wb-18-139
Caldwell, H. N. 1846 wb-13-448
Caldwell, James W. 1845 wb-13-173
Caldwell, Joseph 1832 wb-9-583
Call, Joseph 1847 wb-14-98
Callaghan, Maria 1845 wb-13-228
Callahan, J. (Mrs.) 1847 wb-14-72
Callahan, Philip 1851 wb-15-58
Callendar, Thomas 1852 wb-15-281

Caltharp, William 1837 wb-11-92?
Calvert, Willis 1851 wb-14-563
Cameron, Daniel 1855 wb-16-557
Camp, Armstead 1851 wb-15-83
Camp, George 1835 wb-10-539
Camp, George A. 1848 wb-14-235
Camp, James 1816 wb-7-12
Camp, James 1836 wb-10-619
Camp, James T. 1838 wb-11-481
Camp, Martha 1823 wb-8-270
Campbell, Alexander 1828 wb-9-215
Campbell, Francis 1856 wb-16-617
Campbell, Francis 1856 wb-17-65
Campbell, George W. 1848 wd-14-209
Campbell, James 1823 wb-8-266
Campbell, James 1849 wb-14-433
Campbell, James G. 1838 wb-11-174
Campbell, John 1797 wb-2-59
Campbell, Michael 1830 wb-9-394
Campbell, Michael 1845 wb-13-154
Campbell, Philip 1838 wb-11-506
Campbell, Sarah B. 1854 wb-16-344
Campbell, Thomas 1828 wb-9-220
Campbell, Thomas 1854 wb-16-251
Campbell, Washington 1851 wb-15-30
Campbell, Washington G. 1852 wb-15-344
Campbell, William 1860 wb-18-241
Cannon, Newton 1841 wb-12-236*
Cantrell, Juliet A. D. 1840 wb-12-45*
Cantrell, Juliet A. D. 1852 wb-15-449
Capps, Benjamin 1832 wb-10-57
Capps, John 1858 wb-17-501
Carmack, Aquilla 1819 wb-7-356
Carmack, Daniel 1859 wb-17-618
Carmack, George M. 1851 wb-15-118
Carmacks, Aquilla 1816 wb-4-458
Carnes, Edmond 1798 wb-2-131
Carney, Elijah 1852 wb-15-311
Carney, Vincent 1844 wd-13-45
Carow, Henry 1860 wb-18-318
Carper, McCoy 1851 wb-14-616
Carrington, Wilie 1838 wb-11-474
Carrington, William 1835 wb-10-419
Carrothers, Ezekiel 1794 wb-2-7
Carson, Charles S. 1815 wb-4-347
Carson, N. D. 1850 wb-14-493
Carter, Christopher C. 1824 wb-8-377
Carter, Francis 1852 wb-15-314
Carter, John 1822 wb-8-76
Carter, Mary M. 1861 wb-18-611
Carter, Rachel 1859 wb-17-580
Carter, William 1840 wb-12-89*
Cartright, Patience 1838 wb-11-253
Cartwright, Caleb 1799 wb-2-148
Cartwright, David 1814 wb-4-283

Cartwright, David 1819 wb-7-296
Cartwright, David 1836 wb-10-559
Cartwright, Elizabeth 1857 wb-17-225
Cartwright, Jac 1844 wd-13-29
Cartwright, Jacob 1828 wb-9-247
Cartwright, Jacob 1838 wb-11-170
Cartwright, Jane 1834 wb-10-332
Cartwright, Jefferson 1833 wb-10-236
Cartwright, Pembroke 1826 wb-8-557
Cartwright, Robert 1816 wb-4-471
Cartwright, Robert 1816 wb-7-27
Cartwright, Robt. 1810 wb-4-82
Cartwright, Thomas 1843 wb-12-448*
Cartwright, Vincent 1815 wb-4-352
Caruthers, William B. 1851 wb-15-11
Carvin, William 1808 wb-4-2
Carvin, William 1826 wb-8-561
Case, John 1855 wb-16-568
Casey, James 1849 wb-14-452
Casey, James 1851 wb-14-643
Casey, Sims 1847 wb-14-21
Cassellman, Jacob 1791 wb-1-194
Casselman, Benjamin 1826 wb-8-512
Casselman, Jacob 1806 wb-3-125
Castleman, Andrew 1845 wb-13-145
Castleman, Henry 1850 wb-14-489
Castleman, John 1821 wb-8-15
Catc, Rolen 1813 wb-4-256
Cato, Robert 1816 wb-7-67
Cato, Roland 1816 wb-7-83
Cato, Rowland 1854 wb-16-238
Catron, Felix 1843 wb-12-393*
Catron, Susan M. 1848 wd-14-208
Chadwell, George 1860 wb-18-398
Chadwell, Thomas G. 1847 wb-14-61
Chambless, Thos. G. 1809 wb-4-57
Champ, Asahel 1819 wb-7-311
Chandler, William 1851 wb-14-648
Channing, Penina P.? 1860 wb-18-379
Chapman, Samuel 1826 wb-9-59
Chapouil, Pater 1836 wb-11-98
Charles, Elvira 1854 wb-16-284
Charlton, Benjamin F. 1850 wb-14-556
Charlton, John 1840 wb-11-628
Chauvin, William 1834 wb-10-316
Chavis, Francis 1841 wb-12-156*
Chears, Frances 1841 wb-12-128*
Cheny, Eli 1845 wb-13-204
Cherry, Caleb 1825 wb-8-496
Cherry, Eli 1842 wb-12-376*
Cherry, Pierce W. 1852 wb-15-213
Chickering, John 1858 wb-17-492
Chilcutt, B. F. 1860 wb-18-243
Chilcutt, B. P. 1859 wb-18-53
Childress, Elizabeth 1823 wb-8-198

Childress, John 1811 wb-4-137
Childress, John 1821 wb-8-54
Childress, Mary 1855 wb-16-538
Chiles, John 1817 wb-7-125
Christian, Christopher 1828 wb-9-196
Clark, James 1832 wb-10-40
Claiborne, Myra 1859 wb-18-59
Claiborne, Phil 1829 wb-9-356
Claiborne, Sarah 1827 wb-9-137
Claiborne, Thomas A. 1835 wb-10-524
Claiborne, William F. L. 1832 wb-9-566
Clardy, P. J. 1858 wb-17-495
Clark, Daniel 1821 wb-8-46
Clark, George 1791 wb-1-238
Clark, George H. 1851 wb-15-61
Clark, James 1833 wb-10-264
Clark, Lardner 1802 wb-2-252
Clark, Martin 1859 wb-18-103
Clark, Thomas 1806 wb-3-49
Clark, Thomas H. 1853 wb-15-559
Clark, William 1793 wb-1-261
Clark, William S. 1833 wb-10-162
Clay, John M. 1838 wb-11-213
Clay, John M. 1838 wb-11-262
Clay, Larkin 1817 wb-7-166
Clay, Woodson 1824 wb-8-373
Cleaveland, Mary 1843 wb-12-472*
Clemans, William 1811 wb-4-129
Clemmons, Abgail 1824 wb-8-374
Clemons, Isaac 1853 wb-15-483
Clemons, James 1857 wb-17-232
Clendening, John 1786 wb-1-43
Clifford, Patrick 1829 wb-9-354
Clinard, John 1853 wb-15-540
Clinton, Isaac 1851 wb-14-597
Cloud, Jeremiah 1849 wb-14-415
Cloud, William 1847 wb-14-7
Clow, Mary 1821 wb-7-507
Cloyed, Ezekiel 1847 wb-14-108
Clyne, Mathew 1851 wb-15-207
Coale, Thomas 1814 wb-4-311
Coats, John 1839 wb-11-540
Cobbs, William A. 1851 wb-14-609
Cobler, Davis 1838 wb-11-407
Cochran, Ammon 1844 wd-13-31
Cochran, Lewis 1851 wb-15-5
Cockerell, James 1854 wb-16-221
Cockrell, John 1838 wb-11-200
Cockrell, Richard H. 1838 wb-11-366
Cockrell, William N. 1838 wb-11-363
Cockrill, John jr. 1841 wb-12-189*
Cockrill, Nathaniel 1861 wb-18-420
Coglin, Edward 1821 wb-8-24
Colby, Cyrus 1851 wb-14-606
Coldwell, Joseph 1823 wb-8-253

Cole, Pilmore 1829 wb-9-275
Cole, Pilmore 1844 wb-13-67
Coleman, Joseph 1819 wb-7-312
Coleman, S. K. 1860 wb-18-317
Collins, Thomas 1845 wb-13-278
Collins, Zilpha 1847 wb-14-26
Collinsworth, Alice 1828 wb-9-171
Collinsworth, Edmond 1816 wb-7-5
Collinsworth, Edward 1824 wb-8-392
Collinsworth, William 1795 wb-2-34
Coltard, William 1822 wb-8-150
Coltharp, William 1833 wb-10-96
Compton, William 1845 wb-13-324
Condon, James 1838 wb-11-241
Condon, Rose (Col) 1860 wb-18-326
Cone, Gilum 1856 wb-17-148
Cone, John W. 1854 wb-16-218
Conger, Stephen 1806 wb-3-116
Congo, Stephen 1806 wb-3-107
Conlan, Catharine A. 1857 wb-17-338
Conlon, James 1851 wb-15-70
Conlow, James 1848 wd-14-227
Connell, William P. 1852 wb-15-396
Cook, James H. 1844 wb-13-72
Cook, John 1854 wb-16-277
Cook, John H. 1859 wb-17-574
Cook, Joseph 1840 wb-12-57*
Cook, Sarah 1851 wb-15-196
Cook, Will A. 1842 wb-12-355*
Cook, William A. 1842 wb-12-311*
Cooke, George 1797 wb-2-92
Cooke, William W. 1816 wb-7-90
Coon, Conrad 1843 wb-12-424*
Cooper, Henry 1823 wb-8-179
Cooper, William 1807 wb-3-161
Cooper, William 1817 wb-7-159
Coots, Elizabeth 1826 wb-9-31
Coots, John 1821 wb-8-15
Coots, John 1840 wb-12-97*
Copeland, John 1840 wb-11-617
Copely, John 1847 wb-14-69
Coppage, Thomas L. 1848 wd-14-215
Corbett, William A. 1854 wb-16-362
Corbitt, William 1810 wb-4-99
Corbitt, Wm. 1810 wb-4-109
Cordell, William 1846 wb-13-494
Cotton, Mary 1861 wb-18-567
Cotton, Precilla 1852 wb-15-368
Cotton, Thomas N. 1854 wb-16-348
Coulter, R. 1843 wb-12-394*
Coulter, Robert 1845 wb-13-159
Courtny, Nehimiah 1794 wb-2-4
Cowan, Alexander 1817 wb-7-207
Cowgill, Abner 1826 wb-8-513
Cowgill, Abner 1826 wb-9-19

Cowley, William H. 1860 wb-18-294
Cox, Frances B. 1853 wb-16-61
Cox, Greenberry 1805 wb-3-6
Cox, Herman 1861 wb-18-620
Cox, Jesse 1816 wb-4-457
Cox, Jesse 1816 wb-7-68
Cox, Thomas 1831 wb-9-483
Cox, Washington S. 1848 wb-14-248
Crabb, Henry 1828 wb-9-147
Craddock, Armistead 1852 wb-15-280
Craddock, Asa 1835 wb-10-410
Craddock, Asa 1835 wb-10-486
Crafford, William 1804 wb-2-397
Craighead, Elizabeth 1830 wb-9-362
Craighead, Jane 1851 wb-15-20
Craighead, John B. 1854 wb-16-393
Cravens, John 1803 wb-2-339
Crawford, William A. 1803 wb-2-338
Creal, William 1845 wb-13-214
Creech, Thomas 1861 wb-18-453
Crichler, Branker 1839 wb-11-542
Crichlow, Brasher? 1838 wb-11-161
Criddle, John 1822 wb-8-82
Criddle, John 1832 wb-9-619
Criddle, Livingston G. 1831 wb-9-478
Criddle, Smith 1861 wb-19-31
Criddle, Susannah 1830 wb-9-366
Criddles, Sarah 1834 wb-10-353
Cripps, Christian 1791 wb-1-229
Crisp, Ezekiel 1847 wb-14-26
Crockett, David 1828 wb-9-248
Cross, Marlin 1798 wb-2-121
Cross, Richard 1798 wb-2-121
Cross, Richard 1802 wb-2-262
Cross, William 1826 wb-9-27
Crossway, John N. 1827 wb-9-113
Crossway, Livingston G. 1831 wb-9-484
Crossway, Nicholas 1823 wb-8-206
Crosswy, Linnington 1832 wb-10-53
Crutcher, Edmund 1847 wb-14-5
Crutcher, Foster G. 1851 wb-14-561
Crutcher, Mary Jane 1851 wb-14-660
Crutcher, Thomas 1844 wb-13-76
Crutcher, Thomas H. 1836 wb-10-626
Cullom, Jesse 1838 wb-11-202
Cullum, Jessee 1838 wb-11-208
Cummins, William 1853 wb-15-476
Cunningham, Enoch 1851 wb-15-10
Cunningham, George 1814 wb-4-319
Cunningham, John 1861 wb-18-429
Curfman, William 1833 wb-10-157
Curl, Seth 1839 wb-11-556
Curley, John B. 1853 wb-15-484
Currin, Ann S. 1854 wb-16-417
Currin, John 1830 wb-9-459

Currin, John 1858 wb-17-487
Curry, Robert B. 1849 wb-14-443
Curry, Robert B. 1861 wb-18-433
Curtis, Fanny 1843 wb-12-424*
Curtis, Francis 1827 wb-9-134
Curtis, Francis 1841 wb-12-147*
Curtis, Joshua 1819 wb-7-325
Curtis, Rice 1798 wb-2-139
Cutchen, Joshua 1826 wb-9-37
Cutchen, Samuel 1830 wb-9-440
Cutchin, Mourning 1841 wb-12-175*
Dabbs, Henry B. 1851 wb-15-203
Dabbs, John R. 1847 wb-14-40
Dabbs, Richard 1825 wb-8-483
Dalaney, Henry Rozier 1852 wb-15-283
Dalaney, Henry Rozier 1852 wb-15-284
Dale, Francis H. 1847 wb-14-116
Dally, Joseph G. 1843 wb-13-2
Dance, Russell 1839 wb-11-574
Dancer, Ulric M. 1822 wb-8-96
Daniels, Henry 1855 wb-16-595
Dauge, Enock 1842 wb-12-322*
Dauge, Enock 1842 wb-12-373*
Daughty, George 1847 wb-14-36
David, James 1823 wb-8-278
Davie, Thomas 1798 wb-2-118
Davis, Andrew 1815 wb-4-392
Davis, Andrew 1816 wb-7-7
Davis, Elijah L. 1858 wb-17-478
Davis, Elisha 1803 wb-2-297
Davis, Elisha 1821 wb-8-12
Davis, Enoch 1797 wb-2-95
Davis, Francis 1832 wb-9-619
Davis, Hamelton W. 1838 wb-11-290
Davis, Hatch 1852 wb-15-249
Davis, Howell Tatum 1860 wb-18-376
Davis, Jerome B. 1861 wb-18-480
Davis, John 1824 wb-8-289
Davis, John 1853 wb-16-206
Davis, John E. 1854 wb-16-240
Davis, John W. 1838 wb-11-176
Davis, Joseph 1804 wb-2-379
Davis, Loyd 1847 wb-14-53
Davis, Nancy 1819 wb-7-296
Davis, Polly 1807 wb-3-166
Davis, Robert 1853 wb-15-485
Davis, Samuel 1840 wb-12-89*
Davis, Samuel 1852 wb-15-358
Davis, Sarah 1821 wb-7-505
Davis, Seth 1822 wb-8-125
Davis, Sterling 1832 wb-9-616
Davis, Thomas 1848 wb-14-268
Davis, William 1820 wb-7-454
Davy, Thomas 1797 wb-2-92
Dawsen, John 1800 wb-2-178

Dawson, John 1851 wb-15-22
Dawson, Zacheriah 1800 wb-2-174
DeGrove, Q. C. 1861 wb-18-451
DeGrove, Quincy C. 1861 wb-18-533
DeLaHay, John H. 1860 wb-18-249
Deaderick, George M. 1832 wb-10-56
Deadrick, George M. 1817 wb-7-149
Deadrick, George M. 1851 wb-14-671
Deadrik, John 1798 wb-2-105
Deal, Eliza 1860 wb-18-161
Deal, Elizaeth 1855 wb-16-460
Dean, James 1818 wb-7-224
Dean, Jas. 1802 wb-2-229
Deatheridge, John 1825 wb-8-506
Deathrige, Thomas 1812 wb-4-193
Decker, John 1840 wb-11-626
Deiss, Daniel 1854 wb-16-432
Delee, John 1860 wb-18-214
Deloach, Samuel 1793 wb-1-263
Deloach, Samuel 1813 wb-4-223
Demonbrun, Timothy 1827 wb-9-94
Demoss, Abraham 1851 wb-15-70
Demoss, Abram 1850 wb-14-512
Demoss, Elizabeth K. 1861 wb-19-29
Demoss, James 1814 wb-4-276
Demoss, James 1850 wb-14-487
Demoss, Lewis 1820 wb-7-465
Demoss, Skelton T. 1824 wb-8-357
Dennis, David 1844 wd-13-46
Denny, Elizabeth 1814 wb-4-317
Deshazo, William 1833 wb-10-172
Deshon, Clarissa 1834 wb-10-280
Devault, John 1815 wb-4-378
Dickinson, Catharine R. 1848 wd-14-214
Dickinson, Charles 1807 wb-3-141
Dickinson, Henry 1807 wb-3-147
Dickinson, Henry 1846 wb-13-414
Dickinson, Jacob 1822 wb-8-71
Dickinson, Jacob 1836 wb-10-619
Dickinson, Jacob sr. 1816 wb-7-58
Dickinson, Jane 1807 wb-3-147
Dickinson, John 1815 wb-4-366
Dickinson, William G. 1845 wb-13-183
Dickinson, William T. 1842 wb-12-310*
Dickson, John P. 1845 wb-13-351
Dickson, Joseph 1818 wb-7-223
Dickson, Mary 1816 wb-7-94
Dickson, Sarah 1851 wb-15-191
Dickson, Thomas 1833 wb-10-226
Dickson, William 1816 wb-4-454
Dickson, William 1816 wb-7-86
Dickson, William 1826 wb-9-39
Dickson, William E. 1845 wb-13-351
Dillahunty, John 1798 wb-2-115
Dillahunty, John 1816 wb-4-463

Dillahunty, John 1816 wb-7-19
Dillahunty, John 1817 wb-7-143
Dillahunty, Silas 1829 wb-9-304
Dillahunty, Silas 1842 wb-12-334*
Dillon, Thomas 1814 wb-4-273
Dirickson, Isaiah 1812 wb-4-187
Dismukes, John T. 1847 wb-14-36
Dismukes, Paul 1838 wb-11-439
Dismukes, Paul 1845 wb-13-196
Dismukes, Sarah 1839 wb-12-4
Doak, Samuel 1813 wb-4-237
Dobson, John 1854 wb-16-340
Dobson, William 1860 wb-18-216
Dockerty, William 1852 wb-15-321
Dodson, Allen 1822 wb-8-148
Dodson, Caleb 1848 wd-14-231
Dodson, Frederick 1841 wb-12-124*
Dodson, Timothy 1856 wb-17-99
Doherty, William 1851 wb-15-82
Domidion, Therisa 1843 wb-12-423*
Domidion, Tresed 1847 wb-14-149
Donalson, James 1796 wb-2-45
Donelson, Alexander 1816 wb-7-11
Donelson, Alexander 1834 wb-10-345
Donelson, Charity 1828 wb-9-166
Donelson, Edward B. 1852 wb-15-439
Donelson, Eliza Eleanor 1851 wb-15-195
Donelson, Elizabeth 1828 wb-9-272
Donelson, George 1848 wb-14-238
Donelson, George S. 1851 wb-15-68
Donelson, John 1789 wb-1-109
Donelson, John 1830 wb-9-418
Donelson, Levin 1833 wb-10-238
Donelson, Mary 1849 wb-14-471
Donelson, Mary J. 1843 wb-12-440*
Donelson, Severn 1819 wb-7-330
Donelson, Severn 1838 wb-12-21
Donelson, Stockly 1789 wb-1-91
Donelson, Thomas 1798 wb-2-130
Donelson, William 1829 wb-9-284
Donelson, William sr. 1820 wb-7-404
Donley, Isabel 1838 wb-11-294
Donley, James 1831 wb-9-479
Donley, John 1836 wb-10-551
Donnelly, James 1830 wb-9-456
Dooton, Christian 1790 wb-1-172
Dorris, Elizabeth 1844 wb-13-87
Doshier, Enoch jr. 1851 wb-15-18
Doss, John T. 1851 wb-14-636
Douglas, Elizabeth 1854 wb-16-295
Douglass, Jemima 1845 wb-13-310
Douglass, Tabitha L. 1857 wb-17-269
Douglass, William 1823 wb-8-192
Dove, John 1851 wb-15-60
Downs, James P. 1819 wb-7-360

Downs, John 1860 wb-18-418
Downs, William B. 1846 wb-13-483
Downs, William H. 1854 wb-16-382
Dozier, Enoch 1849 wb-14-390
Dozier, Margaret 1859 wb-17-564
Dozier, William N. 1846 wb-13-456
Drake, B. W. 1859 wb-17-623
Drake, Benjamin 1831 wb-9-513
Drake, Blunt W. 1841 wb-12-222*
Drake, Eli 1831 wb-9-524
Drake, Emila 1820 wb-7-457
Drake, Ephraim 1817 wb-7-123
Drake, Isaac 1815 wb-4-357
Drake, Isaac 1816 wb-7-52
Drake, Isaac 1853 wb-15-480
Drake, J. F. 1838 wb-11-271
Drake, James F. 1838 wb-11-488
Drake, John 1835 wb-10-410
Drake, Jonathan 1801 wb-2-213
Drake, Jonathan 1834 wb-10-375
Drake, Jonathan 1837 wb-11-36
Drake, Joseph 1816 wb-7-11
Drake, Joshua 1857 wb-17-165
Drake, Sevier 1828 wb-9-216
Dreyfous, Isaac 1852 wb-15-356
Dreyfus, Leccy (Lucy?) 1851 wb-14-607
Driver, Abner P. 1853 wb-16-174
Dudley, Thomas E. 1838 wb-11-505
Duff, Robert L. 1833 wb-10-240
Duffield, John 1813 wb-4-234
Duffy, Hetty 1840 wb-11-615
Dunam, Henry 1803 wb-2-289
Dunam, John 1790 wb-1-136
Dungey, John 1843 wb-12-432*
Dunivant, Daniel 1854 wb-16-451
Dunn, Lewis 1845 wb-13-168
Dunn, Michael C. 1854 wb-16-216
Dunn, William A. 1854 wb-16-217
Dunneway, Opie 1830 wb-9-447
Durand, Timothy 1852 wb-15-232
Durard, Timothy 1851 wb-15-121
Eakin, Isabella 1853 wb-15-574
Eakin, Moses 1818 wb-7-257
Eakin, Spencer 1841 wb-12-189*
Eakin, William 1851 wb-14-642
Earhart, Abraham 1854 wb-16-297
Earhart, David 1817 wb-7-168
Earhart, Elijah 1820 wb-7-469
Earhart, Nimrod 1846 wb-13-378
Earheart, Philip 1818 wb-7-218
Earthman, A. J. 1838 wb-11-321
Earthman, Isaac 1835 wb-10-459
Earthman, Isaac F. 1829 wb-9-353
Earthman, John 1828 wb-9-191
Earthman, Lewis 1828 wb-9-255

East, Addison 1838 wb-11-454
East, Benjamin 1809 wb-4-78
East, Henry 1859 wb-17-607
East, Henry C. 1853 wb-15-546
Eastman, E. G. 1861 wb-18-431
Eatherly, Frank 1859 wb-17-571
Edgar, Jno. T. 1861 wb-18-566
Edmiston, Alice 1840 wb-12-94*
Edmiston, David 1816 wb-7-12
Edmiston, John 1816 wb-7-5
Edmiston, Nicholas P. 1835 wb-10-504
Edmiston, Robert 1816 wb-7-51
Edmiston, Thomas 1834 wb-10-290
Edmonds, David W. 1816 wb-7-68
Edmonds, David W. 1818 wb-7-222
Edmondson, James 1852 wb-15-435
Edmondson, Robert 1816 wb-4-449
Edmondson, Thomas 1824 wb-8-365
Edmondson, Thomas 1825 wb-8-435
Edmondson, Thomas 1853 wb-16-78
Edmonson, Eliza V. 1851 wb-15-29
Edney, Amanda 1846 wb-13-413
Edney, Elevin 1853 wb-15-514
Edney, Levin 1852 wb-15-302
Edney, Newton 1835 wb-10-501
Edwards, Arthur 1806 wb-3-71
Edwards, Isaac 1816 wb-7-97
Ehrhart, John 1861 wb-18-430
Elam, Catharine 1839 wb-11-543
Elliot, John 1800 wb-2-176
Ellis, Azariah 1853 wb-16-86
Ellis, Edward 1800 wb-2-175
Ellis, Jeremiah 1845 wb-13-218
Ellis, John H. 1851 wb-14-572
Ellis, Joshua 1840 wb-12-8*
Elliston, Charles M. 1857 wb-17-380
Elliston, John 1823 wb-8-171
Elliston, Joseph J. 1857 wb-17-367
Engleman, Joseph 1816 wb-4-430
Engleman, Joseph 1816 wb-7-13
Engster, John W. 1857 wb-17-150
Erskine, Thomas W. 1850 wb-14-551
Erwin, James sr. 1861 wb-18-589
Erwin, Joseph 1845 wb-13-356
Erwin, William 1838 wb-11-368
Estes, Bartlet 1836 wb-11-106
Estill, John 1837 wb-11-46
Estis, Henson 1840 wb-12-40*
Estis, Martha 1847 wb-14-81
Etheridge, David T. 1823 wb-8-178
Eubank, Ambrose 1860 wb-18-140
Evans, Bird 1814 wb-4-292
Evans, Elizabeth 1820 wb-7-434
Evans, John 1809 wb-4-56
Evans, Joseph S. 1860 wb-18-399

Evans, Margret D. C. 1853 wb-16-91
Evans, Robert 1819 wb-7-312
Evans, W. G. 1841 wb-12-140*
Evans, William G. 1842 wb-12-350*
Everett, James 1818 wb-7-275
Everett, Jesse 1860 wb-18-172
Everett, Jessee J. 1853 wb-16-117
Everett, Kinchen 1835 wb-10-516
Everett, Simon 1830 wb-9-435
Everett, Thomas H. 1854 wb-16-412
Ewell, William C. 1817 wb-7-207
Ewers, William 1851 wb-14-562
Ewin, Watts D. 1857 wb-17-383
Ewing, Alexander 1822 wb-8-98
Ewing, Alexander 1824 wb-8-405
Ewing, Andrew 1813 wb-4-235
Ewing, John L. 1816 wb-4-457
Ewing, John O. 1826 wb-9-49
Ewing, Joseph L. 1860 wb-18-383
Ewing, M. P. 1838 wb-11-286
Ewing, M. P. 1838 wb-11-305
Ewing, Nathan 1830 wb-9-404
Ewing, Nathan 1852 wb-15-414
Ewing, Randall M. 1853 wb-16-130
Ewing, Sarah 1840 wb-12-31
Ewing, Sarah 1841 wb-12-74
Ewing, Sarah 1855 wb-16-592
Ewing, Sarah S. 1859 wb-17-577
Ewing, Susannah 1819 wb-7-292
Ewing, William 1846 wb-13-369
Exum, Arthur 1819 wb-7-332
Ezell, George M. G. 1859 wb-17-621
Ezell, Jeremiah 1838 wb-11-378
Ezell, Lafayette 1852 wb-15-466
Fairfax, Walter 1813 wb-4-253
Falls, James 1834 wb-10-275
Farmbrough, Stewart 1816 wb-7-30
Farquharson, Robert 1857 wb-17-284
Farrar, Landon C. 1829 wb-9-293
Farrer, John 1823 wb-8-275
Farrow, Sebina 1825 wb-8-499
Faulkner, William 1851 wb-14-575
Feeland, Polly 1817 wb-7-164
Feeland, William 1817 wb-7-124
Feland, William 1815 wb-4-346
Felts, Carey 1840 wb-12-50
Felts, Isham 1825 wb-8-457
Felts, William 1859 wb-18-90
Felts, William G. 1860 wb-18-214
Ferebee, Henry 1823 wb-8-183
Ferebee, Thomas 1847 wb-14-5
Ferguson, Henry 1847 wb-14-110
Ferguson, John G. 1860 wb-18-212
Ferguson, William M. 1859 wb-17-573
Ferrill, Bazzill 1851 wb-15-141

Ferris, G. P. 1861 wb-18-588
Fielder, John 1807 wb-3-140
Fielder, John 1818 wb-7-279
Fields, Eli 1834 wb-10-351
Finch, Edward 1832 wb-9-595
Finley, Anthony 1847 wb-14-81
Finn, John 1852 wb-15-316
Finn, Thomas 1833 wb-10-64
Finney, Thomas 1820 wb-7-490
Finney, William 1836 wb-10-620
Fish, James D. 1815 wb-4-355
Fishback, Elijah 1800 wb-2-179
Fisher, Frederick E. 1857 wb-17-295
Fisk, Ebenezer 1853 wb-16-133
Fitzgerald, Jno. M. 1841 wb-12-160*
Fitzhugh, Ezekiel 1824 wb-8-359
Fitzhugh, Lydia 1840 wb-12-1*
Fitzhugh, Samuel 1832 wb-10-12
Fitzhugh, Samuel 1832 wb-9-580
Flannegan, Martin 1860 wb-18-286
Fleming, Thomas S. 1849 wb-14-590
Fletcher, James H. 1814 wb-4-271
Fletcher, James H. 1815 wb-4-373
Flippin, H. G. 1857 wb-17-417
Fly, John D. 1814 wb-4-294
Fly, Sarah 1836 wb-10-548
Fong?, George R. 1846 wb-13-487
Forbs, Benjamin S. 1837 wb-11-73
Ford, A. J. 1851 wb-15-11
Ford, Addison J. 1851 wb-15-18
Ford, Francis P. 1823 wb-8-170
Ford, John L. 1853 wb-15-576
Forgison, William 1796 wb-2-58
Forrest, William M. 1850 wb-14-553
Forsyth, George R. 1844 wb-13-78
Foster, Ann Augusta 1852 wb-15-298
Foster, Anthony 1831 wb-9-491
Foster, Ephraim H. 1854 wb-16-425
Foster, George 1799 wb-2-159
Foster, George 1809 wb-4-78
Foster, George 1853 wb-15-485
Foster, John L. 1852 wb-15-377
Foster, R. C. 1845 wb-13-151
Foster, Robert C. 1845 wb-13-200
Foster, Septemus W. 1839 wb-11-577
Foulks, Craddock 1819 wb-7-294
Foulks, Thomas 1818 wb-7-235
Fow, Jacob 1830 wb-9-372
Fowler, Wiley 1815 wb-4-377
Fowler, William 1828 wb-9-232
Fowlkes, Mary 1827 wb-9-136
Fowlkes, Thomas 1828 wb-9-163
Fraker, John A. 1847 wb-14-29
Frazer, John 1828 wb-9-271
Frazer, William 1828 wb-9-273

Frazior, Mahala C. 1851 wb-14-627
Frazor, Daniel 1819 wb-7-333
Frazor, Rebecca 1836 wb-10-552
Freeland, James 1784 wb-1-16
Freeland, Samuel 1811 wb-4-156
Freeman, Carney 1851 wb-15-206
Freeman, Carra 1850 wb-14-479
Freeman, York 1832 wb-9-596
French, Joseph 1791 wb-1-240
Fry, Frederick 1832 wb-9-618
Fudge, James 1855 wb-16-458
Fulghum, Theophilus 1857 wb-17-229
Fuqua, Gabriel 1823 wb-8-204
Fuqua, John C. 1852 wb-15-376
Fuqua, Rebecca 1853 wb-15-519
Fuqua, Thomas 1860 wb-18-328
Gains, Fountain H. 1816 wb-4-468
Gains, Fountain H. 1816 wb-7-10
Gains, William S. 1816 wb-4-449
Gains, William S. 1816 wb-7-62
Galbraith, John S. 1841 wb-12-43
Gallaspie, David 1803 wb-2-326
Garland, Elisha 1837 wb-11-14
Garland, Samuel 1860 wb-18-376
Garrett, John L. 1845 wb-13-309
Garrett, Lewis R. 1842 wb-12-359*
Garrett, Thomas 1816 wb-7-99
Garrett, Thomas 1832 wb-10-1
Garrett, William 1854 wb-16-350
Garrett, William W. 1832 wb-9-609
Garrett, William sr. 1857 wb-17-365
Gatlin, John M. C. 1853 wb-15-528
Gatlin, Lazerous 1808 wb-4-5
Gatlin, Nathan 1856 wb-16-613
Gaylord, John D. 1860 wb-18-299
Gee, John 1829 wb-9-302
Gee, John 1847 wb-14-25
Gee, John 1848 wb-14-278
Gee, Jonathan 1793 wb-1-274
Gee, Joseph C. 1847 wb-14-161
Gee, Joshua J. 1852 wb-15-351
Gee, Samuel M. 1840 wb-12-32
Gee, William W. 1840 wb-11-615
Geisler, Edward 1858 wb-17-478
Gentry, Nicholas 1784 wb-1-5
Getor, Argolas 1792 wb-1-252
Gibbs, John 1841 wb-12-244*
Gibson, William 1828 wb-9-217
Gibson, William 1843 wb-12-396*
Gilchrist, Sarah Ellen 1851 wb-14-563
Gildusky, Julius 1853 wb-16-79
Giles, Josiah E. 1827 wb-9-133
Gilky, John 1796 wb-2-57
Gill, J. J. 1854 wb-16-214
Gill, James J. 1855 wb-16-586

Gillam, Danl. 1809 wb-4-58
Gillenwaters, John 1806 wb-3-65
Gilliam, Charles 1803 wb-2-303
Gilliam, John 1802 wb-2-230
Gilliam, Nathaniel 1838 wb-11-287
Gilliam, Susan 1828 wb-9-218
Gilliam, Thomas 1853 wb-15-509
Gilliam, William 1852 wb-15-387
Gilliam, Wm. 1804 wb-2-343
Gilliland, Wm. 1800 wb-2-188
Gilman, Timothy W. 1850 wb-14-480
Glasgow, Isaac 1861 wb-18-470
Glasgow, Jesse 1838 wb-11-399
Glasgow, John C. 1843 wb-12-423*
Glass, Samuel F. 1860 wb-18-212
Glaves, Michael 1811 wb-4-155
Gleaves, Absalom 1834 wb-10-394
Gleaves, James 1841 wb-12-250*
Gleaves, James M. 1844 wb-13-65
Gleaves, John G. 1855 wb-16-483
Gleaves, Mathew 1805 wb-3-4
Gleaves, Mathew 1842 wb-12-345*
Gleaves, Michael 1814 wb-4-315
Gleaves, Michael 1834 wb-10-313
Gleaves, Michael H. 1854 wb-16-432
Gleaves, Rachel 1836 wb-10-607
Gleaves, Robert H. 1853 wb-16-116
Gleaves, Thomas 1831 wb-9-519
Gleaves, Thomas 1850 wb-14-490
Gleaves, William 1840 wb-12-15
Gleaves, William D. 1841 wb-12-124*
Glenn, John 1829 wb-9-349
Golsten, Lewis 1858 wb-17-459
Gooch, David R. 1854 wb-16-338
Gooch, Jane 1841 wb-12-249*
Goode, William 1828 wb-9-219
Goodlett, Robert 1858 wb-17-489
Goodrich, Ed 1857 wb-17-418
Goodrich, John 1817 wb-7-214
Goodrich, John 1837 wb-11-32
Goodrich, R. 1838 wb-11-456
Goodrich, William 1847 wb-14-151
Goodwin, Ann 1835 wb-10-465
Goodwin, Ann 1835 wb-10-501
Goodwin, George 1808 wb-4-9
Goodwin, George 1838 wb-11-121
Goodwin, J. U. J. 1847 wb-14-91
Goodwin, James 1835 wb-10-424
Goodwin, Jane T. 1838 wb-11-280
Goodwin, Jesse 1810 wb-4-119
Goodwin, John L. 1825 wb-8-408
Goodwin, Thomas E. 1847 wb-14-13
Goodwin, William 1832 wb-9-604
Goodwin, William W. 1851 wb-15-138
Gordon, James 1859 wb-18-104

Gordon, Margaret T. 1834 wb-10-380
Gossett, Henry 1853 wb-16-202
Gowan, William 1790 wb-1-168
Gowen, Allen 1800 wb-2-166
Gowen, Allen 1800 wb-2-171
Gowen, John 1835 wb-10-503
Gower, Abel B. 1847 wb-14-88
Gower, Alexander K. 1815 wb-4-394
Gower, Charlotte 1860 wb-18-349
Gower, Edith 1822 wb-8-73
Gower, Elijah 1795 wb-2-34
Gower, Elijah 1807 wb-3-161
Gower, Elisha 1853 wb-16-132
Gower, L. F. 1854 wb-16-225
Gower, Manoah 1847 wb-14-24
Gower, Noah 1847 wb-14-36
Gower, William 1852 wb-15-349
Gower, William E. 1815 wb-4-354
Gower, William E. 1831 wb-9-556
Gower, William L. 1830 wb-9-426
Gowine, David 1784 wb-1-7
Graham, Andrew 1822 wb-8-150
Graham, George 1844 wd-13-13
Graham, George 1844 wd-13-47
Graham, George 1853 wb-15-484
Graham, Susanna F. 1838 wb-11-494
Graham, William P. 1861 wb-18-450
Graves, Francis 1798 wb-2-102
Graves, Henry 1826 wb-9-38
Graves, John 1825 wb-8-443
Graves, John 1838 wb-11-467
Graves, John P. 1839 wb-11-570
Graves, Sally 1838 wb-11-172
Graves, Samuel A. 1857 wb-17-162
Graves, U. 1853 wb-15-541
Graves, William H. 1861 wb-18-587
Gray, Benajah 1837 wb-11-43
Gray, Eleanor 1860 wb-18-383
Gray, Elizabeth 1853 wb-16-166
Gray, Henrietta 1838 wb-11-457
Gray, John 1798 wb-2-100
Gray, John 1837 wb-11-53
Gray, Sally 1838 wb-11-466
Gray, Sarah 1838 wb-11-182
Greaves, Francis 1797 wb-2-90
Green, Benjamin 1838 wb-11-376
Green, Evan 1815 wb-4-338
Green, Green B. 1842 wb-12-331*
Green, Greenberry 1842 wb-12-363*
Green, Isaiah D. 1833 wb-10-214
Green, James M. 1855 wb-16-466
Green, Lewis 1806 wb-3-138
Green, Littleton 1814 wb-4-289
Green, Oliver 1832 wb-10-10
Green, Oliver 1848 wb-14-286

Green, Robert 1804 wb-2-395
Greene, Josiah D. 1851 wb-15-117
Greene, William 1836 wb-10-552
Greer, Benjamin 1838 wb-11-380
Greer, George 1833 wb-10-71
Greer, Jackson 1840 wb-12-9*
Greer, John 1803 wb-2-301
Greer, John 1847 wb-14-150
Greer, Martin 1822 wb-8-123
Gregory, Wright 1816 wb-7-92
Gresham, Austin 1837 wb-11-79
Griffin, Derham 1850 wb-14-497
Griffis, Durham 1850 wb-14-497
Griffith, D. 1850 wb-14-497
Grimes, William 1813 wb-4-225
Grisham, J. W. 1861 wb-19-34
Grizard, Edney 1853 wb-16-69
Grizzard, Jeremiah 1832 wb-9-574
Gross, Eveline 1859 wb-17-608
Gross, George S. 1857 wb-17-458
Grundy, Ann P. (Nancy?) 1847 wb-14-66
Grundy, Felix 1841 wb-12-98*
Grundy, Felix 1856 wb-17-77
Gubbins, Wm. 1786 wb-1-59
Gulledge, William 1825 wb-8-452
Gulliford, James 1849 wb-14-468
Guthrie, Henry 1838 wb-11-291
Guthrie, Henry 1852 wb-15-394
Gwathmey, John B. 1818 wb-7-256
Gwin?, Lewis 1785 wb-1-26
Hackney, Danl. 1803 wb-2-330
Hadley, William 1842 wb-12-334*
Hadley, William 1842 wb-12-368*
Hadley, William 1845 wb-13-140
Hagar, George 1858 wb-17-533
Hagar, George W. 1859 wb-18-88
Hager, Henry 1847 wb-14-46
Haggard, John 1793 wb-1-283
Haggard, John 1794 wb-2-4
Haggert, John 1803 wb-2-309
Hail, Thomas 1814 wb-4-272
Haile, Meshach 1813 wb-4-243
Hale, Francis 1847 wb-14-81
Hale, Meshack 1847 wb-14-70
Hale, Nicholas 1843 wb-12-389*
Hale, Thomas J. 1845 wb-13-169
Hale, William C. 1848 wd-14-216
Haley, William 1845 wb-13-179
Haley, William 1851 wb-15-54
Hall, Charles M. 1827 wb-9-98
Hall, Clem 1824 wb-8-387
Hall, Edward 1858 wb-17-491
Hall, Hampton 1856 wb-17-84
Hall, John H. 1841 wb-12-168*
Hall, Nancy B. 1830 wb-9-376

Ham, Samuel 1855 wb-16-480
Hamilton, Eleazor 1793 wb-1-282
Hamilton, George 1796 wb-2-45
Hamilton, George 1798 wb-2-114
Hamilton, James 1816 wb-4-456
Hamilton, James 1816 wb-7-46
Hamilton, James 1851 wb-14-624
Hamilton, John 1857 wb-17-383
Hamilton, Joseph D. 1857 wb-17-197
Hamilton, Nancy J. 1859 wb-17-618
Hamilton, Sally B. 1854 wb-16-284
Hamilton, William 1847 wb-14-92
Hampton, Sally B. 1861 wb-18-596
Hancock, John 1817 wb-7-207
Hanes, Thomas G. 1856 wb-17-101
Hanks, R. H. 1853 wb-16-61
Hanna, James 1817 wb-7-167
Hanna?, James 1841 wb-12-44
Hannah, John 1854 wb-16-312
Hannah, Joseph 1810 wb-4-120
Harbeson, Robert 1851 wb-14-636
Hardgrave, Francis 1828 wb-9-246
Hardgraves, Sarah 1832 wb-10-38
Hardgraves, Skelton 1828 wb-9-204
Hardin, Jeremiah 1798 wb-2-117
Harding, Amelia E. 1860 wb-18-223
Harding, David M. 1854 wb-16-427
Harding, Elizabeth 1816 wb-7-57
Harding, F. Jefferson 1861 wb-18-451
Harding, George 1850 wb-14-526
Harding, Giles 1810 wb-4-105
Harding, Giles 1843 wb-12-405*
Harding, Henry 1850 wb-14-525
Harding, Henry P. 1848 wb-14-251
Harding, Thomas 1805 wb-3-35
Harding, William 1833 wb-10-72
Harding, William 1848 wd-14-232
Hardy, Anne 1811 wb-4-126
Hardy, Elizabeth 1822 wb-8-72
Hardy, Henson 1816 wb-4-423
Hardy, Henson 1816 wb-7-23
Hardy, Jinny 1811 wb-4-126
Hardy, Rebecca K. 1827 wb-9-117
Hardy, Thomas 1816 wb-4-408
Hardy, Thomas 1816 wb-7-18
Hargrave, John 1799 wb-2-144
Harmand, Anthony 1793 wb-1-274
Harness, Elizabeth J. 1859 wb-17-619
Harney, Sarah 1851 wb-15-119
Harper, William 1822 wb-8-75
Harper, Williamson 1818 wb-7-219
Harris, Adam G. 1841 wb-12-146*
Harris, Anne 1822 wb-8-107
Harris, David 1827 wb-9-120
Harris, Edwin 1847 wb-14-59

Harris, Elizabeth 1854 wb-16-276
Harris, Ezra 1846 wb-13-451
Harris, G. W. 1848 wd-14-219
Harris, George W. 1849 wb-14-421
Harris, Howell 1809 wb-4-49
Harris, Jacob 1813 wb-4-209
Harris, Jno. H. 1861 wb-18-565
Harris, Lucinda 1847 wb-14-150
Harris, Moody 1819 wb-7-357
Harris, Moses B. 1851 wb-14-657
Harris, Pyre 1809 wb-4-28
Harris, Rosana C. 1852 wb-15-364
Harris, Thomas F. 1852 wb-15-210
Harris, Thomas G. 1857 wb-17-158
Harris, Thomas K. 1816 wb-7-1
Harris, Tyre 1813 wb-4-209
Harris, Tyree 1802 wb-2-266
Harris, William 1846 wb-13-365
Harris, William 1848 wd-14-227
Harris, William sr. 1848 wb-14-177
Harris, Wyatt 1853 wb-15-529
Harrison, Frankey 1851 wb-15-6
Harrison, John 1794 wb-1-313
Harrison, John 1838 wb-11-309
Harrison, Richard 1795 wb-2-14
Harrison, Richard R. 1850 wb-14-528
Harrison, Rolla 1858 wb-17-453
Harrison, Thomas 1821 wb-7-513
Harrison, Thos. 1809 wb-4-46
Harrisson, Lewis 1819 wb-7-360
Harrod, James 1784? wb-1-16
Hart, Anthony 1795 wb-2-19
Hart, George 1841 wb-12-130*
Hart, John 1842 wb-12-320*
Hart, Samuel 1832 wb-10-36
Hartman, George 1840 wb-12-49*
Harwood, John 1823 wb-8-169
Haskins, Chancy T. 1838 wb-11-323
Haslam, Samuel 1858 wb-17-555
Hatch, Lemuel 1804 wb-2-397
Hatcher, Ward 1841 wb-12-209*
Hathaway, George 1827 wb-9-111
Hauser, John H. 1855 wb-16-534
Hawkins, Elizabeth M. 1851 wb-14-615
Hawkins, Willis N. 1850 wb-14-536
Hay, Ann 1814 wb-4-291
Hay, Ann 1826 wb-9-21
Hay, David 1801 wb-2-205
Hay, John 1808 wb-4-14
Hay, John G. 1835 wb-10-513
Hayes, Oliver B. 1859 wb-17-631
Hayes, Sarah 1831 wb-9-560
Hayes, William 1811 wb-4-125
Hayes, William 1811 wb-4-157
Haynie, John N. 1823 wb-8-172

Hays, Blackman 1847 wb-14-105
Hays, Charles 1854 wb-16-385
Hays, James 1832 wb-10-32
Hays, John 1841 wb-12-34
Hays, Sally 1826 wb-9-58
Hays, Sam 1793 wb-1-286
Hays, William 1836 wb-10-537
Hays, William S. 1861 wb-18-605
Hays, Wm. 1787 wb-1-67
Hays, Zachariah 1816 wb-7-52
Haywood, John 1827 wb-9-82
Hazcl, Samuel K. 1833 wb-10-157
Head, Thurston 1827 wb-9-118
Hearn, Ebenezer 1835 wb-10-420
Heaton, Amos 1795 wb-2-13
Heaton, Amos 1814 wb-4-308
Heaton, Amos 1860 wb-18-263
Heaton, Elizabeth 1805 wb-3-33
Heaton, Robert 1844 wb-13-9
Heaton, Thomas 1853 wb-15-534
Hebron, John 1837 wb-11-78
Henderson, Adam 1853 wb-15-538
Henderson, Richard H. 1845 wb-13-191
IIenderson, William Y. 1858 wb-17-487
Hendricks, William P. 1854 wb-16-226
Hennon, James 1821 wb-7-509
Hennon?, James 1831 wb-9-559
Henry, William 1844 wb-13-108
Herbert, Nathaniel 1821 wb-8-25
Heriges, John J. 1858 wb-17-456
Herndon, Joseph 1860 wb-18-144
Herndon, Joseph 1860 wb-18-166
Herrin, John F. 1851 wb-15-176
Herrin, William 1854 wb-16-239
Heslip, Joseph 1833 wb-10-116
Hetzel, George 1851 wb-14-643
Hewitt, Caleb 1817 wb-7-141
Hewlett, George 1822 wb-8-72
Hewlett, William 1834 wb-10-338
Hewlitt, Edmond 1819 wb-7-330
Hickman, Edwin 1791 wb-1-223
Hickman, Edwin 1808 wb-3-197
Hickman, John P. 1841 wb-12-27
Hickman, John R. 1852 wb-15-458
Hickman, Thomas 1851 wb-15-144
Hickman, Thomas 1853 wb-16-113
Hickman, William 1811 wb-4-132
Hicks, Edward D. 1840 wb-12-60*
Hicks, Mary 1804 wb-2-388
Hiett, Moses 1833 wb-10-161
Higginbotham, John 1842 wb-12-277*
Higgins, Hannah 1861 wb-18-593
Hiland, James 1794 wb-1-313
Hill, H. R. W. 1854 wb-16-448
Hill, John 1859 wb-17-630

Hill, John R. 1860 wb-18-134
Hill, Reuben S. 1858 wb-17-509
Hill, Samuel 1857 wb-17-226
Hill, Thomas 1824 wb-8-303
Hill, William 1830 wb-9-396
Hill, William 1838 wb-11-212
Hines, James D. 1846 wb-13-466
Hinton, James 1807 wb-3-157
Hitchens, Joseph 1857 wb-17-160
Hitt, Reuben S. 1857 wb-17-231
Hobbs, C. S. 1849 wb-14-432
Hobbs, Collin S. 1831 wb-9-493
Hobbs, Collin S. 1854 wb-16-375
Hobbs, Edward D. 1833 wb-10-178
Hobbs, Thomas 1851 wb-15-89
Hobbs, Thomas W. 1860 wb-18-297
Hobson, John 1838 wb-11-119
Hobson, Joseph 1843 wb-12-415*
Hobson, William 1816 wb-4-451
Hobson, William 1816 wb-7-37
Hodge, Francis 1828 wb-9-195
Hodge, George 1834 wb-10-381
Hodge, George 1835 wb-10-423
Hodge, James 1818 wb-7-234
Hogan, John 1860 wb-18-224
Hogan, Robert 1854 wb-16-451
Hogan, Thomas 1844 wb-13-127
Hoggatt, Abraham 1825 wb-8-428
Hoggatt, Diana 1828 wb-9-218
Hoggatt, Dianna 1829 wb-9-337
Hoggatt, John 1824 wb-8-381
Holeman, John 1848 wb-14-276
Hollinsworth, Charles 1833 wb-10-238
Hollinsworth, Elizabeth 1856 wb-17-280
Hollis, Joshua 1798 wb-2-110
Hollis, Richard S. B. 1831 wb-9-542
Holloway, John 1836 wb-10-609
Holmes, Hannah 1830 wb-9-359
Holmes, Sarah 1841 wb-12-16
Holmes, William 1830 wb-9-401
Holt, Jacob 1804 wb-2-378
Holt, Jacob 1804 wb-2-381
Holton, Samuel 1853 wb-16-90
Homes, John 1832 wb-9-578
Homes, William 1831 wb-9-499
Hommedien, Richard F. L. 1847 wb-14-67
Hooker, Anne 1808 wb-3-199
Hooper, Absolom 1813 wb-4-246
Hooper, C. Y. 1849 wb-14-472
Hooper, Churchell 1808 wb-4-19
Hooper, Churchwell 1808 wb-4-17
Hooper, Claborne G. 1848 wb-14-259
Hooper, Ennis 1801 wb-2-200
Hooper, James 1832 wb-10-51
Hooper, James A. 1855 wb-16-541

Hooper, James H. 1841 wb-12-10
Hooper, Jesse 1841 wb-12-242*
Hooper, Joseph 1825 wb-8-454
Hooper, Martha 1825 wb-8-462
Hooper, Thomas 1826 wb-8-556
Hooper, Thomas 1826 wb-9-35
Hooper, William C. 1847 wb-14-39
Hoover, Philip 1831 wb-9-519
Hope, Adam 1842 wb-12-258*
Hope, Adam 1842 wb-12-274*
Hope, Adam 1842 wb-12-364*
Hope, Ann 1838 wb-11-270
Hope, John 1805 wb-3-17
Hope, John 1816 wb-7-91
Hope, Samuel W. 1848 wd-14-187
Hopkins, Martha A. 1861 wb-19-2
Horton, James 1861 wb-18-503
Horton, Joseph W. 1847 wb-14-51
Horton, Josiah 1828 wb-9-168
Hough, Joseph H. 1844 wd-13-16
House, George W. 1851 wb-15-116
House, R. 1859 wb-18-60
House, Rosa 1861 wb-18-548
Houser, J. G. 1851 wb-15-127
Houser, Johanna C. 1857 wb-17-355
Houser, John G. 1853 wb-16-124
Houston, James B. 1824 wb-8-359
Houston, James B. 1837 wb-11-39
Howard, Amelia 1858 wb-17-490
Howell, William H. 1859 wb-18-51
Howerton, Eldred 1857 wb-17-172
Howlett, Isaac H. 1834 wb-10-304
Howlett, James 1831 wb-9-550
Howlett, Stockley H. 1835 wb-10-420
Howlett, William 1831 wb-9-535
Howlett, William 1832 wb-9-590
Hows, Racy 1859 wb-17-629
Hudgen, W. D. 1852 wb-15-353
Hudgins, W. D. 1858 wb-17-433
Hudson, Cuthbert 1853 wb-16-210
Hudson, Harry 1857 wb-17-258
Hudson, Isaac 1850 wb-14-489
Hudson, Judith 1853 wb-16-201
Huffman, Balsor 1843 wb-12-433*
Huggins, C. G. 1853 wb-15-577
Huggins, Eli C. 1858 wb-17-506
Huggins, John 1855 wb-16-542
Huggins, William 1857 wb-17-280
Hugh, J. H. 1846 wb-13-422
Hughes, John L. 1855 wb-16-467
Humble, Mac 1860 wb-18-287
Hume, Alfred 1854 wb-16-277
Hume, William 1833 wb-10-179
Humphries, John 1851 wb-14-660
Hundley, Margarett 1841 wb-12-117*

Hunt, A. J. 1854 wb-16-313
Hunt, Enoch J. 1852 wb-15-247
Hunt, Tibman S. 1838 wb-11-333
Hunt, William G. 1834 wb-10-314
Hunt, William Hasell 1841 wb-12-230*
Hunter, David 1859 wb-18-87
Hunter, David 1861 wb-18-579
Hunter, Jacob 1807 wb-3-159
Hunter, John 1789 wb-1-95
Hurst, Elijah 1816 wb-7-13
Hurst, William 1816 wb-7-11
Hurt, Benjamin 1860 wb-18-145
Hurt, Floyd 1842 wb-12-299*
Hurt, Floyd 1855 wb-16-539
Hurt, Hiram 1817 wb-7-206
Hurt, Josiah 1818 wb-7-239
Hurt, Josiah 1835 wb-10-429
Hutchings, Thomas 1805 wb-3-5
Hutson, Jessee 1804 wb-2-344
Hutton, Charles 1814 wb-4-269
Hutton, Thomas W. 1847 wb-14-115
Hyde, C. H. 1855 wb-16-525
Hyde, Christiana H. 1857 wb-17-342
Hyde, Edmund 1851 wb-14-560
Hyde, Edmund J. 1845 wb-13-324
Hyde, Henry 1812 wb-4-200
Hyde, Henry 1825 wb-8-422
Hyde, Jordan 1828 wb-9-154
Hyde, L. C. 1860 wb-18-381
Hyde, Mary D. 1836 wb-10-541
Hyde, Rebecca 1829 wb-9-347
Hyde, Richard 1859 wb-17-598
Hyde, Richard sr. 1859 wb-18-44
Hyde, Taswell 1838 wb-11-401
Hynes, Andrew 1849 wb-14-469
Ingram, Samuel B. 1858 wb-17-427
Ingram, Thomas 1807 wb-3-175
Iredale, John 1842 wb-12-260*
Ireson, James 1788 wb-1-69
Irwin, John 1816 wb-7-19
Irwin, Rachel 1861 wb-18-635
Jackson, Andrew 1845 wb-13-291
Jackson, Carril 1829 wb-9-296
Jackson, Craven 1821 wb-8-33
Jackson, Henry 1818 wb-7-218
Jackson, Jessee 1811 wb-4-163
Jackson, John 1803 wb-2-277
Jackson, John B. 1816 wb-7-50
Jackson, John T. 1851 wb-15-88
Jackson, Mary W. 1847 wb-14-137
Jackson, Nelson P. 1831 wb-9-505
Jackson, Sarah 1803 wb-2-276
Jackson, Stephen 1813 wb-4-249
Jackson, William 1833 wb-10-197
Jackson, William 1840 wb-11-616

Jackson, William 1850 wb-14-523
James, Elizabeth 1851 wb-15-167
James, George W. 1851 wb-14-635
James, Henry F. 1842 wb-12-308*
James, Mary T. 1851 wb-15-166
James, Thomas 1825 wb-8-500
Jenkins, A. 1861 wb-18-473
Jenkins, Alexander 1861 wb-19-2
Jennings, Jonathan 1784 wb-1-7
Jennings, Obadiah 1832 wb-10-58
Jennings, Sophia 1851 wb-14-680
Jennings, William 1851 wb-15-102
Jerow, George Fredrick 1819 wb-7-319
Jewell, John 1814 wb-4-270
Jewell, Joseph 1822 wb-8-131
Johns, John 1860 wb-18-237
Johns, John Sr. 1827 wb-9-83
Johnson, Elenor 1858 wb-17-537
Johnson, Isaac 1839 wb-11-593
Johnson, Jonathan 1816 wb-7-41
Johnson, Joseph 1838 wb-11-245
Johnson, Joseph H. 1841 wb-12-51
Johnson, Oliver 1816 wb-4-466
Johnson, Richard 1844 wb-13-12
Johnson, Samuel C. 1845 wb-13-348
Johnson, Thomas 1842 wb-12-361*
Johnson, William 1828 wb-9-228
Johnson, William H. 1852 wb-15-389
Johnston, Ermin 1824 wb-8-340
Johnston, Exum 1814 wb-4-280
Johnston, Exum 1816 wb-4-422
Johnston, Exum 1816 wb-7-14
Johnston, H. R. 1852 wb-15-323
Johnston, John 1857 wb-17-185
Johnston, Michael 1850 wb-14-556
Johnston, Oliver 1816 wb-7-69
Jones, A. S. 1860 wb-18-226
Jones, Amzi 1843 wb-12-436*
Jones, Armour 1859 wb-18-64
Jones, C. A. 1846 wb-13-433
Jones, Cecelia A. 1847 wb-14-10
Jones, Daniel 1815 wb-4-384
Jones, David 1806 wb-3-98
Jones, Edmond 1851 wb-15-89
Jones, Edward 1851 wb-15-123
Jones, Elizabeth 1816 wb-4-424
Jones, Elizabeth 1816 wb-7-19
Jones, Elizabeth 1838 wb-11-194
Jones, Isaac 1857 wb-17-228
Jones, Isaac M. 1855 wb-16-567
Jones, Jarvis 1844 wd-13-46
Jones, Richard R. 1823 wb-8-186
Jones, William 1850 wb-14-497
Jonnard, Edward 1860 wb-18-382
Jonte, Frederic 1858 wb-17-531

Jonte, Peter 1840 wb-12-90*
Jordan, Drewry 1836 wb-10-632
Jordan, Louisa 1857 wb-17-161
Jordan, Meredith 1831 wb-9-486
Jordan, Sarah 1859 wb-18-86
Jordan, Williamson 1847 wb-14-163
Jordon, Benjamin 1847 wb-14-103
Joslin, Lewis 1856 wb-17-126
Joslin, Richard 1829 wb-9-355
Jost, Christiana 1850 wb-14-511
Jost, Thomas 1850 wb-14-522
Jourdan, Meredith 1831 wb-9-468
Joyce, Joseph T. 1852 wb-15-417
Joyce, Thomas 1838 wb-11-116
Karnes, Mathew 1817 wb-7-165
Keeling, George 1819 wb-7-326
Keeling, George 1841 wb-12-223*
Keeling, Leonard 1833 wb-10-152
Kellum, Henry 1799 wb-2-154
Kellum, John 1826 wb-9-56
Kellum, William 1811 wb-4-165
Kelly, Francis 1851 wb-15-58
Kelly, J. S. 1859 wb-18-49
Kenedy, Henry 1802 wb-2-239
Kenedy, James 1802 wb-2-262
Kennedy, John 1785 wb-1-39
Kennedy, Lemuel 1822 wb-8-112
Keor, Saml. 1809 wb-4-38
Kerney, Vincent 1844 wb-13-89
Kerr, Samuel 1811 wb-4-164
Keuthman, H. A. 1843 wb-12-439*
Keuthman, Henry A. 1846 wb-13-365
Key, Elizabeth 1830 wb-9-368
Key, William 1830 wb-9-366
Key, William W. 1820 wb-7-481
Keys, William 1835 wb-10-401
Kezer, Timothy 1845 wb-13-296
Kimbro, John 1852 wb-15-413
King, Delia C. 1858 wb-17-520
King, James 1847 wb-14-165
King, Lewis 1827 wb-9-122
King, Robert 1860 wb-18-132
King, Sarah 1857 wb-17-414
King, Sarah 1861 wb-18-531
King, Thomas 1852 wb-15-235
King, Thomas S. 1852 wb-15-256
King, William 1808 wb-4-16
King, William 1848 wd-14-196
Kirby, John M. 1849 wb-14-457
Kirk, Pamela 1861 wb-18-427
Kirkman, Thomas 1827 wb-9-127
Kirkpatrick, John 1806 wb-3-136
Knight, Graves 1838 wb-11-403
Knight, Graves 1838 wb-11-409
Knight, John 1833 wb-10-205

Knight, Margaret 1836 wb-11-33
Knight, Moses 1836 wb-10-618
Knight, Nicholas 1856 wb-17-85
Knox, Benjamin 1806 wb-3-51
Knox, James 1826 wb-9-35
Knox, Mary C. 1829 wb-9-298
Koen, Daniel 1812 wb-4-198
Koen, Lemuel 1805 wb-3-30
Koen, Ruben 1802 wb-2-252
Koonce, James H. 1816 wb-4-420
Koonce, John 1807 wb-3-175
Kuhn, Francis 1853 wb-16-134
Lambert, Mathew 1848 wb-14-234
Lane, Denny 1846 wb-13-399
Lane, Denny 1847 wb-14-34
Lane, Thomas 1825 wb-8-441
Lane, Thomas 1837 wb-11-20
Langford, Nancy 1859 wb-18-52
Langham, John 1809 wb-4-74
Lanier, Buchanan H. 1830 wb-9-443
Lapsley, Catharine R. 1844 wb-13-122
Laramore, Edward 1781 wb-1-6
Larken, William T. 1854 wb-16-417
Lassiter, Rachel 1859 wb-17-628
Lassiter, William 1836 wb-10-550
Laurence, Timothy D. 1830 wb-9-397
Laurents, Alexander 1853 wb-16-163
Lawrence, Alexander 1851 wb-15-77
Lawrence, Amanda E. 1861 wb-18-545
Lawrence, Ann E. 1859 wb-18-52
Lawrence, William P. 1853 wb-16-73
Lay, John 1841 wb-12-200*
Lay, Thomas 1836 wb-10-599
Lazenby, Alexander 1839 wb-11-530
Lea, John 1851 wb-15-203
Leake, Joseph C. 1860 wb-18-249
Leake, Sarah 1860 wb-18-194
Leddon, Benjamin 1815 wb-4-328
Lee, Braxton 1841 wb-12-151*
Lee, Catharine 1856 wb-17-144
Lee, John 1815 wb-4-339
Lee, John 1820 wb-7-469
Lee, Lewis H. 1815 wb-4-341
Lefever, Cathrine 1785 wb-1-41
Lemar, William 1811 wb-4-157
Lenear, William 1814 wb-4-314
Lenox, Samuel 1822 wb-8-145
Lentz, Jacob 1851 wb-15-61
Lesley, Peter 1848 wb-14-241
Lester, German 1850 wb-14-511
Lester, John 1820 wb-7-370
Letten, Lemuel 1814 wb-4-319
Letton, Lemuel 1815 wb-4-337
Leverton, Thomas 1817 wb-7-160
Levingston, William 1839 wb-11-602

Levy, William 1824 wb-8-335
Lewis, Benjamin F. 1828 wb-9-228
Lewis, Benjamin F. 1839 wb-11-612
Lewis, Joel 1817 wb-7-139
Lewis, Micajah G. 1826 wb-8-530
Lewis, Richard 1857 wb-17-156
Lewis, Samuel 1793 wb-1-292
Lewis, William T. 1820 wb-7-423
Lewis, William T. Sr. 1805 wb-3-3
Lewis, William Terrell jr. 1813 wb-4-229
Liddell, J. H. 1861 wb-18-430
Lidden, Benjamin 1803 wb-2-332
Lightholder, Christopher 1789 wb-1-96
Lindley, Philip 1857 wb-17-375
Linn, John E. 1826 wb-9-36
Lippencut, William 1809 wb-4-43
Little, Henry 1814 wb-4-305
Little, Henry 1814 wb-4-314
Littlefield, E. B. 1836 wb-10-631
Litton, Joseph 1847 wb-14-13
Littrell, Winney F. 1842 wb-12-299*
Livingston, Eleanor R. 1841 wb-12-149*
Livingston, James 1843 wb-12-478*
Livingston, Rachael 1844 wd-13-22
Livingston, William 1841 wb-12-28
Llenier, William 1812 wb-4-198
Llewallen, Abednego 1790 wb-1-136
Lock, Stephen 1819 wb-7-356
Lockbey, James 1851 wb-15-14
Lockett, Pleasant 1794 wb-2-8
Lockett, Thomas 1795 wb-2-18
Lockhart, John 1842 wb-12-270*
Lockhart, Mary 1859 wb-18-117
Logan, Thomas 1825 wb-8-487
Logue, Eleanor 1831 wb-9-497
Logue, John 1793 wb-1-293
Loller, Lawrence 1793 wb-1-285
Long, P. W. 1851 wb-15-183
Long, Wm. 1803 wb-2-306
Loomis, S. H. 1856 wb-17-104
Love, Amelia 1855 wb-16-495
Love, Charles J. 1838 wb-11-210
Love, David B. 1851 wb-15-172
Love, David B. 1851 wb-15-175
Love, Henry J. 1824 wb-8-376
Love, James T. 1851 wb-15-167
Love, James T. 1852 wb-15-319
Love, Joseph 1831 wb-9-558
Love, William 1845 wb-13-253
Lovel, Jacob 1804 wb-2-373
Lovell, John M. 1856 wb-16-612
Low, John 1793 wb-1-291
Lowe, Bridget 1858 wb-17-440
Lowe, Gideon H. 1854 wb-16-366
Lowe, John 1816 wb-4-441

Lowe, John 1816 wb-7-66
Lowery, Overton 1842 wb-12-325*
Lowry, Absolom 1811 wb-4-160
Lowthen, George 1841 wb-12-165*
Loyons, John B. 1850 wb-14-486
Lucas, Andrew 1830 wb-9-371
Lucas, David 1786 wb-1-46
Lucas, Edmund C. 1861 wb-18-427
Lucas, Harriet 1837 wb-11-53
Lucas, Robert 1797 wb-2-64
Luper, James 1784 wb-1-10
Luster, Thos. J. 1838 wb-11-491
Luton, King 1861 wb-18-468
Lynch, Hugh 1830 wb-9-410
Lynch, John B. 1842 wb-12-325*
Lynch, John B. 1842 wb-12-332*
Lyon, James M. 1857 wb-17-181
Lyon, Merritt 1852 wb-15-460
Lytle, William 1839 wb-11-538
Lytle, William 1851 wb-14-623
Mabry, George W. 1853 wb-16-185
Maclin, James C. 1803 wb-2-273
Maclin, William 1803 wb-2-275
Maclin, William sr. 1798 wb-2-121
Maclin, Zackfield 1803 wb-2-273
Macon, Betsy 1808 wb-3-191
Maddox, William 1810 wb-4-106
Madole, John W. 1841 wb-12-156*
Maguire, Charles P. 1859 wb-17-620
Mallory, Phillip 1857 wb-17-318
Malloy, Philip 1854 wb-16-392
Man, Mary 1854 wb-16-297
Manifee, Jonas 1822 wb-8-83
Manifee, Thomas 1816 wb-7-61
Mann, William C. 1827 wb-9-80
Manning, Eliza G. 1851 wb-14-603
Manning, Elizio G. 1848 wb-14-274
Marable, James 1851 wb-15-43
Mares, Joseph (MD) 1844 wd-13-17
Mark, Lucy 1815 wb-4-332
Markham, J. P. 1859 wb-18-62
Markham, John P. 1859 wb-18-109
Marlin, George W. 1859 wb-18-52
Marlin, John 1827 wb-9-133
Marling, John L. 1857 wb-17-350
Marrs, William C. 1827 wb-9-80
Marshall, Elihu 1829 wb-9-351
Marshall, Francis H. 1851 wb-14-604
Marshall, Gilbert 1801 wb-2-209
Marshall, Harriet D. 1853 wb-15-509
Marshall, James 1837 wb-11-72
Marshall, Joseph H. 1845 wb-13-336
Marshall, Margaret 1855 wb-16-538
Martin, Brice 1857 wb-17-401
Martin, Edward 1840 wb-11-634

Martin, George 1860 wb-18-318
Martin, George 1860 wb-18-348
Martin, James 1846 wb-13-368
Martin, Prince 1816 wb-4-433
Martin, Prince 1816 wb-7-6
Martin, Samuel 1793 wb-1-292
Martin, Sarah S. (Thomas) 1814 wb-4-283
Martin, Thomas 1802 wb-2-225
Martin, Thomas 1836 wb-10-639
Marton, Campbell 1836 wb-10-552
Mason, Caleb 1841 wb-12-178*
Massey, E. D. 1858 wb-17-561
Masterson, Thomas 1812 wb-4-189
Mathews, Charles 1819 wb-7-294
Mathews, Elizabeth 1851 wb-14-672
Mathews, Hortio 1834 wb-10-373
Mathews, James S. 1853 wb-16-60
Mathews, William 1816 wb-4-456
Mathias, Isiah 1818 wb-7-259
Mathis, Allen 1848 wd-14-229
Mathis, William 1816 wb-7-53
Mathis, William H. 1855 wb-16-563
Matlock, William 1845 wb-13-250
Matlock, William 1848 wd-14-192
Matthews, Thomas 1846 wb-13-400
Maxey, William 1823 wb-8-267
Maxey, William P. 1851 wb-14-588
Maxwell, Francis 1861 wb-18-471
Maxwell, James 1826 wb-9-40
Maxwell, Jesse 1857 wb-17-307
May, A. J. 1852 wb-15-211
May, Eliza F. 1854 wb-16-309
May, Francis 1818 wb-7-220
May, James F. 1844 wd-13-32
May, Philip 1803 wb-2-346
May, Philip 1804 wb-2-374
Mayfield, Isaac 1796 wb-2-44
Mayfield, Isaac 1796 wb-2-50
Mayfield, Isaac 1856 wb-17-108
Mayfield, Isaac 1856 wb-17-55
Mayfield, Sutherlin 1789 wb-1-94
Mayo, John 1811 wb-4-163
Mayo, Samuel 1841 wb-12-13
Mays, James F. 1854 wb-16-404
Mays, Samuel 1838 wb-11-398
Mays, William W. 1853 wb-15-556
Mayson, F. M. 1846 wb-14-4
McAlister, Melton G. 1855 wb-16-514
McAsee, James 1855 wb-16-512
McAsee?, James 1851 wb-14-670
McBean, Daniel 1815 wb-4-385
McBride, James 1821 wb-7-511
McBride, James 1823 wb-8-176
McBride, James 1857 wb-17-248
McBride, Joseph 1815 wb-4-376

McBride, Joseph 1829 wb-9-353
McBurnie, James 1860 wb-18-229
McCain, John 1817 wb-7-142
McCall, A. W. 1861 wb-19-32
McCana, William N. 1852 wb-15-356
McCance, E. W. 1852 wb-15-462
McCarmack, George W. 1854 wb-16-335
McCasland, John 1848 wd-14-229
McChesney, William 1818 wb-7-232
McClain, Thomas 1789 wb-1-95
McClanahan, Henry 1858 wb-17-477
McClendon, Dennis 1844 wb-13-131
McCollum, William 1815 wb-4-322
McCombs, Alexander 1826 wb-8-546
McConnell, Sarah P. 1821 wb-8-32
McConnell, Sarah T. 1821 wb-8-13
McCormac, Andrew 1820 wb-7-411
McCormack, George 1851 wb-15-179
McCormick, James 1842 wb-12-277*
McCown, James 1795 wb-2-35
McCrory, Catharine 1847 wb-14-138
McCrory, Robert 1795 wb-2-33
McCrory, Robert 1796 wb-2-44
McCrory, Robert E. 1843 wb-12-441*
McCullock, David 1818 wb-7-237
McCulough, David 1818 wb-7-257
McCurdy, John L. 1831 wb-9-515
McCutchen, Grizle 1822 wb-8-78
McCutchen, John 1789 wb-1-92
McCutchen, John E. 1838 wb-11-292
McCutchen, John W. 1831 wb-9-466
McCutchen, William 1789 wb-1-93
McCutchin, John 1842 wb-12-323*
McCutchin, John 1842 wb-12-363*
McDaniel, John 1837 wb-11-72
McDaniel, Mary 1855 wb-16-585
McDaniel, Neal 1826 wb-9-65
McEwen, John A. 1859 wb-17-627
McEwen, Joseph H. 1857 wb-17-196
McFadden, Guy 1836 wb-10-582
McFadden, Jane 1851 wb-14-626
McFarland, Anderson 1855 wb-16-479
McFarland, Robert P. 1822 wb-8-111
McFarlin, Thomas 1796 wb-2-40
McGaugh, William 1790 wb-1-128
McGavock, David 1838 wb-11-492
McGavock, David 1842 wb-12-315*
McGavock, Hugh W. 1854 wb-16-296
McGehee, George W. 1830 wb-9-411
McGuiggin, Terrence A. 1822 wb-8-73
McIlwain, Henry 1829 wb-9-276
McIndoe, Robert 1839 wb-11-569
McIntosh, John 1860 wb-18-170
McIver, John 1853 wb-16-203
McKain, John 1816 wb-7-42

McKaw, Wm. 1809 wb-4-58
McKay, Dickinson 1846 wb-13-404
McKay, Duncan 1849 wb-14-399
McKay, Francis 1828 wb-9-177
McKay, Mary 1854 wb-16-413
McKennie, Zanina H. 1856 wb-17-273
McKeon, Miles 1845 wb-13-192
McLarin, Archibald 1829 wb-9-298
McLaughlin, John 1848 wb-14-260
McLaughlin, William H. 1854 wb-16-328
McLaurine, George W. 1832 wb-9-577
McLean, Laughlen 1816 wb-7-66
McLean, Lauhlin 1816 wb-4-469
McLelland, John 1852 wb-15-329
McLemore, Atkins Jefferson 1805 wb-3-15
McLendon, Simon 1809 wb-4-44
McLin, Sarah 1851 wb-14-581
McMahan, James 1854 wb-16-385
McManus, James 1816 wb-4-472
McMeans, John 1806 wb-3-132
McMinn, Nancy 1858 wb-17-477
McMinn, Robert 1845 wb-13-264
McMonin, Dominic 1802 wb-2-230
McMurray, Charles 1845 wb-13-267
McMurry, Samuel 1839 wb-11-547
McMurry, William 1842 wb-12-295*
McNairy, Boyd 1857 wb-17-369
McNairy, Francis 1812 wb-4-171
McNairy, James 1844 wb-13-123
McNairy, John 1838 wb-11-297
McNairy, John N. 1845 wb-13-318
McNairy, John S. 1851 wb-14-661
McNairy, Nathaniel A. 1852 wb-15-309
McNally, Michael 1859 wb-18-172
McNamara, Bryan M. 1854 wb-16-245
McNeil, John 1838 wb-11-146
McNeill, Call 1827 wb-9-94
McNeill, William 1844 wd-13-42
McWhirter, Mary 1817 wb-7-167
McWilliams, Andrew 1835 wb-10-402
Mead, Martha 1851 wb-15-173
Mead, Michael 1852 wb-15-369
Meadows, Jeremiah 1854 wb-16-424
Meaney, Jane 1838 wb-11-431
Meany, Gregory F. 1818 wb-7-281
Mears, Joseph 1844 wd-13-27
Meddor, Jerimiah 1852 wb-15-277
Meek, James 1847 wb-14-12
Meek, Joseph 1838 wb-11-451
Meek, Robert 1845 wb-13-280
Meek, Sarah 1842 wb-12-253*
Menees, James 1837 wb-11-80
Meneese, John 1849 wb-14-409
Menefee, John B. 1832 wb-9-622
Menefee, Jonas 1824 wb-8-337

Menifee, John B. 1830 wb-9-418
Menifee, William N. 1824 wb-8-366
Meredith, John D. 1852 wb-15-465
Merritt, Thomas F. 1840 wb-12-17
Merryman, Alexander 1857 wb-17-181
Merryman, William 1819 wb-7-297
Miles, Bedford W. 1858 wb-17-486
Miles, Hardy D. 1846 wb-13-381
Miles, Samuel 1843 wb-12-391*
Miller, Joseph 1847 wb-14-126
Miller, Lucy 1857 wb-17-283
Miller, Thomas 1858 wb-17-479
Miller, William T. 1860 wb-18-416
Mills, Jacob 1789 wb-1-95
Minnick, Ann 1850 wb-14-493
Minnick, Joseph P. 1835 wb-10-514
Minton, A. E. 1857 wb-17-402
Minton, Thomas B. 1855 wb-16-563
Mitchel, Marget 1788 wb-1-77
Mitchel, Robert 1803 wb-2-317
Mitchel, William 1806 wb-3-49
Mitchell, Hardy 1838 wb-11-389
Mitchell, Wm. 1805 wb-3-42
Moles, Richard P. 1860 wb-18-298
Molloy, Thomas 1802 wb-2-245
Moncrieff, James 1824 wb-8-380
Monday, Gilbert 1830 wb-9-433
Monger, Thomas 1814 wb-4-321
Monroe, Adeline 1855 wb-16-457
Montgomery, A. H. 1858 wb-17-455
Montgomery, Lemuel P. 1814 wb-4-308
Montgomery, Lemuel P. 1837 wb-11-68
Moody, Benjamin 1811 wb-4-151
Moody, Benjn. 1811 wb-4-133
Moody, W. J. 1841 wb-12-114*
Moore, C. C. 1861 wb-18-511
Moore, David 1822 wb-8-121
Moore, Edwin S. 1838 wb-11-437
Moore, Elizabeth 1844 wd-13-14
Moore, James 1786 wb-1-47
Moore, James D. 1845 wb-13-258
Moore, James E. 1853 wb-16-174
Moore, John 1827 wb-9-137
Moore, Joseph 1842 wb-12-333*
Moore, Joseph 1842 wb-12-359*
Moore, Josephus A. 1843 wb-13-1
Moore, Matilda 1861 wb-18-513
Moore, Robert J. 1849 wb-14-447
Moore, Robert J. 1851 wb-15-198
Moore, Sarah F. 1842 wb-12-312*
Moore, Susan 1854 wb-16-338
Moore, Thomas J. 1829 wb-9-311
Moore, William C. 1844 wb-13-49
Morgan, Benjamin 1843 wb-12-442*
Morgan, Frances 1842 wb-12-367*

Morgan, James 1852 wb-15-377
Morgan, Robert F. 1846 wb-13-390
Morgan, Thomas B. 1836 wb-10-635
Morgan, Thomas R. 1836 wb-10-631
Moring, William 1815 wb-4-353
Morris, Daniel 1815 wb-4-345
Morris, Daniel 1816 wb-7-63
Morris, E. C. 1851 wb-14-661
Morris, E. S. 1838 wb-11-509
Morris, Eli 1854 wb-16-396
Morris, Henry B. 1859 wb-18-107
Morris, Isaac E. 1851 wb-15-83
Morris, J(esse) E. 1838 wb-11-120
Morris, Jane 1855 wb-16-511
Morris, Jessee 1803 wb-2-309
Morris, Joseph 1812 wb-4-181
Morris, Martha H. 1860 wb-18-401
Morris, Peter B. 1855 wb-16-558
Morris, Simeon 1803 wb-2-301
Morris, Simon 1804 wb-2-347
Morris, Thomas 1828 wb-9-174
Morris, William P. 1849 wb-14-398
Morrison, Andrew 1832 wb-10-35
Morriss, Jessee 1803 wb-2-272
Morriss, Thomas 1811 wb-4-150
Morton, Asa 1816 wb-7-21
Morton, Henry 1838 wb-11-473
Morton, John 1851 wb-15-129
Moseley, Jephtha 1854 wb-16-434
Moseley, John 1837 wb-11-75
Moseley, Thomas 1820 wb-7-369
Moss, Benjamin 1815 wb-4-364
Moss, Benjamin 1817 wb-7-169
Moss, Danl. 1783 wb-1-25
Moss, David 1845 wb-13-160
Moss, George W. 1847 wb-14-56
Mothershed, John Jett 1815 wb-4-338
Mulhall, Jane 1860 wb-18-375
Mulherrin, James 1826 wb-9-29
Mullen, Elizabeth 1844 wd-13-43
Mullen, Jesse 1821 wb-8-17
Mullen, Jessee 1806 wb-3-136
Mullen, Josiah 1825 wb-8-501
Mullen, William Scott 1810 wb-4-108
Murphy, William 1838 wb-11-476
Murray, Rosanna 1821 wb-7-506
Murray, William 1858 wb-17-456
Murry, Henry 1804 wb-2-391
Nall, John L. 1847 wb-14-119
Nance, Elizabeth V. 1844 wb-13-117
Nance, John S. 1841 wb-12-221*
Nance, William H. 1838 wb-11-362
Nash, Francis 1805 wb-3-1
Nash, Jno. 1802 wb-2-253
Neal, Martha A. 1861 wb-18-616

Neal, Richard P. 1840 wb-12-9*
Neeley, Nancy C. 1853 wb-16-57
Neely, Jane 1827 wb-9-119
Neely, John 1816 wb-7-11
Neely, John 1816 wb-7-58
Neely, Samuel 1845 wb-13-193
Neely, Samuel 1856 wb-17-112
Neely, Thomas 1798 wb-2-131
Neely, Thomas 1847 wb-14-161
Neely, Thos. 1802 wb-2-232
Neely, William 1790 wb-1-166
Neely, William 1842 wb-12-314*
Neese, Jane 1854 wb-16-252
Neill, Call W. 1832 wb-10-20
Neill, John W. 1833 wb-10-100
Nelson, Alexr. 1800 wb-2-194
Nelson, Geo. 1803 wb-2-328
Nelson, Jarrot 1822 wb-8-150
Nelson, Levina 1804 wb-2-393
Neusom, William E. 1831 wb-9-494
New, John 1833 wb-10-270
New, Martin 1848 wb-14-239
Newell, Jane 1831 wb-9-481
Newland, Isaac 1838 wb-11-120
Newland, John 1851 wb-15-122
Newland, Mary 1845 wb-13-290
Newland, Susan 1847 wb-14-100
Newsom, Eliza H. 1833 wb-10-180
Newsom, Priscilla 1849 wb-14-430
Newsom, William B. 1847 wb-14-102
Newsom, William E. 1845 wb-13-176
Newsome, Francis 1845 wb-13-171
Newton, Frederick 1844 wb-13-103
Newton, George 1807 wb-3-162
Newton, George 1807 wb-3-170
Nichol, John 1853 wb-16-68
Nichol, Josiah 1833 wb-10-175
Nichol, Josiah D. 1842 wb-12-300*
Nichol, Mary E. 1845 wb-13-304
Nichols, George 1851 wb-15-83
Nichols, John 1817 wb-7-162
Nichols, John 1860 wb-18-235
Nichols, Sarah 1821 wb-7-508
Nicholson, Boyd M. 1856 wb-17-127
Nicholson, Elijah 1852 wb-15-226
Nicholson, Elisha 1849 wb-14-412
Nicholson, R. G. 1856 wb-17-107
Nicholson, R. M. sr. 1856 wb-17-106
Nicholson, Robert G. 1858 wb-17-464
Nicholson, William 1857 wb-17-227
Noel, Reuben 1850 wb-14-494
Noles, Corbin 1823 wb-8-207
Noles, Lucy 1856 wb-16-614
Nolin, Abraham 1815 wb-4-345
Norman, Leven 1810 wb-4-104

Norment, James 1845 wb-13-154
Norment, William T. 1827 wb-9-84
Northern, Marget 1808 wb-3-221
Northern, Peggy 1813 wb-4-256
Northington, Sterling 1818 wb-7-225
Norvell, Hendrick 1838 wb-11-206
Norvell, Joseph 1847 wb-14-108
Norvell, Joseph 1860 wb-18-331
Norvell, Lipscomb 1843 wb-12-415*
Norwood, Nathaniel 1861 wb-18-619
Nowland, Thos. 1788 wb-1-68
Noy, Jacob 1803 wb-2-299
O'Brien, Charles R. 1852 wb-15-243
O'Neil, John F. 1842 wb-12-354*
Ogden, Benjamin Wesley 1854 wb-16-339
Ogilvie, Harris 1824 wb-8-289
Ogilvie, William 1860 wb-18-352
Oglesby, Elisha 1783 wb-1-4
Oldham, Charles 1817 wb-7-125
Oldham, Peter 1824 wb-8-339
Oliver, Edward 1809 wb-4-30
Oliver, Enoch 1816 wb-7-7
Oliver, Peter 1856 wb-17-57
Orton, Samuel R. 1838 wb-11-302
Osborne, William 1817 wb-7-149
Overall, William 1793 wb-1-283
Overall, William 1795 wb-2-17
Overman, Nancy 1841 wb-12-121*
Overton, Archibald W. 1857 wb-17-475
Overton, James G. 1829 wb-9-303
Overton, John 1833 wb-10-149
Overton, Penelope 1844 wb-13-11
Overton, Samuel 1823 wb-8-260
Overton, Thomas 1824 wb-8-356
Owen, Benjamin 1802 wb-2-225
Owen, Edmond 1822 wb-8-79
Owen, Edmund 1835 wb-10-525
Owen, Frederick 1834 wb-10-384
Owen, James B. 1820 wb-7-377
Owen, James J. 1844 wd-13-22
Owen, Joshua 1820 wb-7-412
Owen, Martha A. R. 1845 wb-13-182
Owen, Mary S. 1838 wb-11-183
Owen, Mary S. 1839 wb-11-553
Owen, Peter 1855 wb-16-595
Owen, Robert C. 1828 wb-9-169
Owen, Sandy 1829 wb-9-351
Owen, Sarah 1837 wb-11-22
Owen, Silas L. 1847 wb-14-170
Owens, Jno. H. 1838 wb-11-158
Pack, Benjamin 1818 wb-7-284
Pack, Thomas 1855 wb-16-594
Pack, Thomas L. 1855 wb-16-602
Page, Absolom 1823 wb-8-205
Page, Frederick D. 1848 wd-14-213

Page, Giles H. 1851 wb-15-120
Page, Henrietta 1860 wb-18-241
Page, Martha 1853 wb-16-62
Page, William 1853 wb-15-511
Page, William B. 1857 wb-17-336
Pankey, Danl 1803 wb-2-348
Pankey, John 1804 wb-2-369
Parham, James 1808 wb-3-218
Parham, Newsom 1840 wb-12-73*
Parham, Peyton 1819 wb-7-324
Parham, William 1815 wb-4-337
Parish, Joel 1798 wb-2-125
Parish, Jolly 1838 wb-11-499
Parker, A. G. 1846 wb-13-371
Parker, Charles L. 1848 wb-14-184
Parker, David 1848 wb-14-174
Parker, Isham A. 1821 wb-8-40
Parker, James E. 1833 wb-10-229
Parker, Jesse 1845 wb-13-245
Parker, Jesse 1845 wb-13-300
Parker, Jesse J. 1857 wb-17-301
Parker, Martha 1809 wb-4-32
Parker, Mary 1833 wb-10-70
Parker, O. F. 1855 wb-16-515
Parker, Sarah E. 1858 wb-17-474
Parker, Susan 1852 wb-15-437
Parker, William 1819 wb-7-306
Parker, William 1843 wb-12-461*
Parks, Joseph 1834 wb-10-376
Parmer, Thomas J. 1824 wb-8-385
Parmontier, Nicholas S. 1835 wb-10-512
Parradise, William 1833 wb-10-131
Parradise, William 1833 wb-10-81
Parrish, Absalom 1836 wb-10-598
Parrish, James S. 1841 wb-12-161*
Parrish, Jessey 1854 wb-16-237
Parrish, Sarah J. 1857 wb-17-324
Parrish, Thomas H. 1851 wb-15-126
Parrish, Woodson 1833 wb-10-154
Parthman, John 1826 wb-8-547
Pate, John W. 1861 wb-18-583
Patterson, Ellen 1858 wb-17-518
Patterson, Jane 1807 wb-3-161
Patterson, John 1819 wb-7-355
Patterson, John 1838 wb-11-442
Patterson, John P. 1848 wd-14-188
Patterson, Mathew 1839 wb-11-531
Patterson, Nathan 1819 wb-7-311
Patterson, Robert 1800 wb-2-164
Patterson, Sarah S. 1846 wb-13-430
Patton, Mathew 1839 wb-11-583
Payne, Albert G. 1861 wb-18-505
Payne, Dorothea 1851 wb-15-184
Payne, George 1813 wb-4-238
Payne, Greenwood 1798 wb-2-118

Payne, John 1858 wb-17-443
Payne, Josiah 1806 wb-3-80
Payne, Mathew sr. 1806 wb-3-124
Payne, Rewben 1838 wb-11-471
Payne, Sarah 1804 wb-2-397
Payne, Sarah 1814 wb-4-315
Payne, Sarah 1841 wb-12-164*
Payne, Squire 1816 wb-7-51
Payne, William 1815 wb-4-383
Peabody, John 1822 wb-8-71
Peabody, John 1851 wb-15-90
Peach, James 1851 wb-15-87
Pearce, Martin 1838 wb-11-400
Pearcy, Maria 1847 wb-14-153
Peas, Wm. B.? 1791 wb-1-217
Peay, Elias 1851 wb-14-620
Peay, George 1845 wb-13-216
Peay, Nancy 1851 wb-14-593
Peck, Caroline 1851 wb-15-56
Peebles, Nathan 1813 wb-4-237
Peebles, Nathan 1818 wb-7-284
Pegram, Francis 1855 wb-16-456
Pegram, George S. 1848 wd-14-191
Pegram, Thomas 1847 wb-14-35
Pegram, William 1840 wb-12-7*
Pemberton, William 1841 wb-12-226*
Pennington, Graves 1854 wb-16-295
Pennington, James T. 1854 wb-16-330
Pennington, William R. 1855 wb-16-559
Pennis, John 1807 wb-3-162
Percy, Charles B. 1851 wb-15-205
Perkins, Nicholas 1801 wb-2-199
Perkins, Peter 1816 wb-7-100
Perkins, Powhattan 1853 wb-15-558
Perkins, Susan 1836 wb-10-616
Perkins, Susannah 1836 wb-10-547
Perkins, Thomas H. 1820 wb-7-474
Perkins, Thomas H. 1827 wb-9-89
Perkins, William 1822 wb-8-104
Perry, Burrell 1852 wb-15-251
Perry, Ester 1858 wb-17-429
Perry, Mary 1858 wb-17-455
Perry, Pamelia 1851 wb-15-114
Perry, Robert 1825 wb-8-495
Petway, Honchey 1857 wb-17-321
Phelps, William 1857 wb-17-152
Philips, Benj. A. 1855 wb-16-597
Philips, Benjamin 1820 wb-7-397
Philips, John 1818 wb-7-276
Philips, Mark 1821 wb-8-16
Philips, Merrell 1831 wb-9-485
Philips, Philip 1797 wb-2-85
Philips, Philip 1817 wb-7-120
Philips, Samuel 1823 wb-8-273
Philips, Samuel L. 1819 wb-7-331

Phillips, David 1798 wb-2-105
Phillips, Joseph 1822 wb-8-119
Phillips, Merrell 1809 wb-4-43
Phillips, Nancy 1841 wb-12-2
Phillips, William 1808 wb-3-224
Phillips, William J. 1861 wb-19-23
Phipps, Nancy 1854 wb-16-298
Phipps, Richardson 1847 wb-14-39
Phips, Ruth 1815 wb-4-333
Pierce, Elizabeth 1841 wb-12-119*
Pierce, Martin 1838 wb-11-400
Pigg, James 1847 wb-14-104
Pigg, Nelson W. G. 1833 wb-10-80
Pigg, Pierson P. 1835 wb-10-481
Pigg, William P. 1833 wb-10-160
Pigue, Mariah 1845 wb-13-187
Pike, James M. 1836 wb-10-573
Pillow, John 1793 wb-1-292
Pillow, John 1794 wb-1-313
Pimmo, Elizabeth 1859 wb-17-635
Pinchum, John 1857 wb-17-178
Pinhard, Thomas 1847 wb-14-41
Pinkard, Thomas 1859 wb-17-566
Pinkerton, David 1842 wb-12-378*
Pipkin, Thomas B. 1820 wb-7-413
Pirie, Alexander 1850 wb-14-554
Pittman, Asa 1838 wb-11-206
Player, Thomas T. 1853 wb-16-274
Player, Thomson T. 1855 wb-16-528
Plummer, James R. 1859 wb-17-615
Poindexter, G. C. 1861 wb-18-473
Pointer, John 1854 wb-16-219
Polk, James K. 1851 wb-14-585
Poltz, Sally 1859 wb-18-49
Pope, John 1838 wb-11-474
Pope, Opie 1860 wb-18-267
Pope, Thadeus 1830 wb-9-400
Porter, Alexander 1833 wb-10-186
Porter, Alexander 1853 wb-16-189
Porter, George 1823 wb-8-251
Porter, James 1817 wb-7-210
Porter, James 1829 wb-9-320
Porter, John 1786 wb-1-45
Porter, Robert 1833 wb-10-225
Porter, Robert M. 1857 wb-17-294
Porterfield, Francis 1834 wb-10-271
Porterfield, Robert R. 1846 wb-13-463
Post, George W. 1859 wb-17-578
Powell, Ann 1837 wb-11-76
Powell, Benjamin R. 1838 wb-11-381
Powell, Dempsey 1832 wb-10-8
Powell, Edmund L. 1842 wb-12-307*
Powell, John T. 1860 wb-18-146
Powell, Lemuel B. 1857 wb-17-415
Poyner, Henry W. 1854 wb-16-352

Poyzer, Benjamin 1833 wb-10-85
Poyzer, George 1818 wb-7-283
Pratt, Samuel 1855 wb-16-453
Preston, Sarah J. 1847 wb-14-27
Price, John 1815 wb-4-331
Price, John C. 1854 wb-16-347
Price, Maria 1861 wb-18-428
Price, Silas 1851 wb-15-169
Prichard, Benjamin 1826 wb-8-554
Prichard, Sarah 1839 wb-11-517
Pride, John 1813 wb-4-254
Priestley, Franklin 1842 wb-12-362*
Priestley, James 1821 wb-8-1
Priestley, Sarah 1829 wb-9-303
Priestley, William 1820 wb-7-459
Prior, Zachariah B. 1838 wb-11-274
Pritchard, Benjamin 1826 wb-9-33
Pritchett, Benjamin 1826 wb-9-47
Pritchett, Ephraim 1822 wb-8-159
Probarts, William Y. 1820 wb-7-371
Pryor, Saml. 1811 wb-4-130
Pucket, Cheatham 1811 wb-4-146
Pugh, Elizabeth 1834 wb-10-350
Pugh, John 1816 wb-4-410
Pugh, John 1816 wb-7-21
Pugh, John 1835 wb-10-434
Pugh, Saml. 1834 wb-10-372
Pugsley, Charles 1832 wb-9-596
Pulley, David 1819 wb-7-359
Pulley, Robert M. 1853 wb-16-191
Purdy, Robert 1832 wb-10-38
Pyle, Benjamin 1845 wb-13-148
Quarles, Wm. P. 1809 wb-4-59
Quigley, Patrick 1784 wb-1-17
Quinn, Michael 1841 wb-12-176*
Quisenberry, Henry 1831 wb-9-466
Quisenberry, Lucinda 1848 wb-14-279
Rains, John 1835 wb-10-404
Rains, John 1857 wb-17-154
Rains, Martha 1837 wb-11-70
Rains, Naomi 1821 wb-8-18
Rains, Ursula 1857 wb-17-301
Rains, William 1812 wb-4-199
Rains, William 1827 wb-9-102
Ralston, David 1831 wb-9-546
Ramsay, Jacob W. 1828 wb-9-167
Ramsey, David 1806 wb-3-116
Ramsey, David 1806 wb-3-135
Ramsey, John 1852 wb-15-359
Ramsey, William 1790 wb-1-169
Ramsey, William 1790 wb-1-176
Ramsey, William 1834 wb-11-519
Ramsey, William sr. 1840 wb-12-53*
Randal, Aquila 1837 wb-11-6
Randall, Anna 1822 wb-8-77

Randall, Micha 1823 wb-8-201
Randolph, Peter 1819 wb-7-359
Randolph, William Y. 1830 wb-9-410
Rape, Daniel 1838 wb-11-507
Rape, Susanah M. 1846 wb-13-403
Rascoe, Alexander 1857 wb-17-282
Raworth, Edward 1836 wb-10-587
Ray, William 1849 wb-14-413
Raymer, Susan 1860 wb-18-402
Raymond, N. T. 1851 wb-14-557
Raymond, Nicholas 1813 wb-4-257
Read, Francis N. 1830 wb-9-417
Read, Hezekiah 1806 wb-3-118
Read, Jones 1829 wb-9-346
Read, Jones 1839 wb-11-590
Read, Nancy 1851 wb-14-575
Read, Robert 1816 wb-4-429
Read, Wiats 1805 wb-3-34
Reaves, Daniel 1824 wb-8-375
Redmond, Arthur 1822 wb-8-140
Reed, Jessee 1797 wb-2-79
Reed, Jessee 1798 wb-2-111
Reeves, Elanor 1852 wb-15-443
Rice, Elisha 1807 wb-3-175
Rice, Hiram 1857 wb-17-151
Rice, John 1792 wb-1-249
Rice, John 1806 wb-3-107
Richards, Elizabeth 1855 wb-16-478
Richards, Henry 1847 wb-14-90
Richards, James L. 1859 wb-18-54
Richards, Joaly 1847 wb-14-40
Richardson, David M. 1828 wb-9-210
Richardson, Elizabeth 1821 wb-8-29
Richardson, James 1824 wb-8-358
Richardson, James B. 1853 wb-16-181
Richardson, Milley 1842 wb-12-333*
Richardson, Nancy 1840 wb-12-31
Richardson, William 1847 wb-14-132
Richmond, Winifred 1854 wb-16-397
Ridley, Geo. 1793 wb-1-281
Ridley, George 1838 wb-11-139
Ridley, James 1847 wb-14-131
Ridley, James 1857 wb-17-210
Ridley, Samuel J. 1828 wb-9-153
Rieger, John 1815 wb-4-390
Riggon, John 1857 wb-17-177
Rigney, Isaac 1814 wb-4-270
Rineman, Susan 1833 wb-10-235
Rineman, Susan 1844 wb-13-62
River, Jacob 1851 wb-15-86
Roach, Aaron 1838 wb-11-297
Roach, Ann 1836 wb-11-29
Roach, Hannah 1835 wb-10-534
Roach, James C. 1850 wb-14-487
Roach, Jesse 1848 wd-14-198

Roach, Lydia 1848 wb-14-173
Roach, Stephen 1816 wb-4-430
Roach, Stephen 1816 wb-7-8
Roach, William 1845 wb-13-231
Roane, Ann 1831 wb-9-502
Roane, James 1833 wb-10-200
Roane, James 1833 wb-10-251
Roberts, Adam 1802 wb-2-255
Robertson, A. B. 1842 wb-12-265*
Robertson, Burrell 1850 wb-14-555
Robertson, Charles 1806 wb-3-67
Robertson, Christopher 1832 wb-10-54
Robertson, Duncan 1833 wb-10-225
Robertson, Elijah 1797 wb-2-77
Robertson, Elijah 1859 wb-17-615
Robertson, Jonathan F. 1815 wb-4-381
Robertson, Lydia 1833 wb-10-68
Robertson, Mark 1784 wb-1-53
Robertson, Mark C. C. 1830 wb-9-417
Robertson, Mark C. C. 1841 wb-12-229*
Robertson, Nowell H. 1836 wb-10-546
Robertson, Sarah 1847 wb-14-34
Robinson, Jane P. 1848 wb-14-182
Robinson, Thomas C. 1832 wb-9-595
Robinson, William 1833 wb-10-237
Robinson, William P. 1815 wb-4-344
Robinson, William P. 1825 wb-8-461
Robinson, William P. 1848 wb-14-241
Roland, Elizabeth 1818 wb-7-232
Rosser, David 1853 wb-16-120
Roulston, David 1838 wb-11-334
Rowans, Daniel 1801 wb-2-223
Rowe, James S. 1836 wb-10-539
Rowland, Joseph 1828 wb-9-179
Ruddle, Cornelius 1787 wb-1-54
Russell, Alfred H. 1844 wb-13-135
Russell, D. W. 1858 wb-17-532
Russell, Hannah 1854 wb-16-263
Russell, James 1820 wb-7-370
Russell, James 1843 wb-12-436*
Russell, Thomas 1824 wb-8-319
Rutledge, Henry M. 1844 wb-13-83
Rutledge, Henry M. 1844 wd-13-14
Ryan, Darby 1852 wb-15-438
Ryan, Darby 1852 wb-15-441
Ryver, Jacob 1851 wb-14-644
Saddler, James 1851 wb-15-42
Sadler, Burwell 1810 wb-4-118
Sadler, James M. 1851 wb-15-66
Sadler, Jeremiah 1852 wb-15-315
Sadler, Lucy 1833 wb-10-238
Sadler, Mary 1833 wb-10-238
Sadler, Thomas 1849 wb-14-287
Saffarans, Catharine 1856 wb-17-91
Saffarans, David 1853 wb-15-573

Salisbury, William 1807 wb-3-177
Sample, Robert 1823 wb-8-268
Samuel, Richard 1851 wb-14-590
Sanders, John 1820 wb-7-370
Sanders, Thomas 1812 wb-4-200
Sanderson, Edward 1826 wb-9-64
Sanderson, Robert 1825 wb-8-448
Sanderson, William 1808 wb-3-211
Sandhouse, Lambert 1857 wb-17-196
Sandy, William 1841 wb-12-127*
Santee, Michael 1810 wb-4-102
Sappington, Francis B. 1800 wb-2-178
Sappington, Francis B. 1818 wb-7-254
Sappington, Mark B. 1795 wb-2-28
Saunders, Francis 1821 wb-7-510
Saunders, John W. 1842 wb-12-335*
Saunders, William 1847 wb-14-22
Savage, George E. 1854 wb-16-313
Savage, James 1857 wb-17-378
Sayre, Foster 1820 wb-7-453
Scales, Henry 1845 wb-13-351
Scales, James T. 1855 wb-16-519
Scales, Joseph 1833 wb-10-261
Scales, Nicholas H. 1849 wb-14-457
Scales, Robert 1853 wb-16-115
Scales, Sarah P. 1853 wb-16-127
Schattels, Simon 1857 wb-17-357
Schnee, Gotfred 1856 wb-17-91
Schorr, Henry 1857 wb-17-310
Schorr, Lewis 1851 wb-15-130
Schuman, Frederick 1829 wb-9-287
Sconce, Matilda 1854 wb-16-314
Sconce, Thomas M. 1853 wb-16-94
Scott, Ann 1852 wb-15-412
Scott, Jane 1841 wb-12-122*
Scott, Mary 1822 wb-8-128
Scott, Thomas 1841 wb-12-243*
Scott, Walter 1857 wb-17-155
Scott, William 1813 wb-4-255
Scruggs, Edward 1859 wb-18-63
Scruggs, Langhorn 1841 wb-12-106*
Seaborn, John H. 1841 wb-12-235*
Seaborne, John H. 1852 wb-15-255
Seabourn, Benjamin 1813 wb-4-245
Searcy, Robert 1820 wb-7-470
Searcy, Robert E. 1823 wb-8-172
Searcy, Robert E. 1834 wb-10-308
Searcy, Sarah 1842 wb-12-313*
Sears, Green H. 1847 wb-14-60
Seat, Hartwell 1827 wb-9-135
Seat, Nathl. 1802 wb-2-268
Seck, Simeon 1846 wb-13-400
Seibert, George 1859 wb-17-609
Selgreaves, Joseph A. 1792 wb-1-247
Settler, James W. 1826 wb-8-552

Shaffer, Richd. 1793? wb-1-295
Shain, Morris 1821 wb-8-14
Shane, Elenor 1842 wb-12-251*
Shane, Morris 1823 wb-8-282
Shane, Morris 1836 wb-11-109
Shane, Moses 1838 wb-11-331
Shane, Penelope 1843 wb-12-433*
Shane, Rebecca B. 1853 wb-15-482
Shannon, J. C. 1861 wb-19-17
Shannon, Samuel 1811 wb-4-161
Sharpe, Benjamin 1848 wb-14-247
Sharrenburger, Caspar 1854 wb-16-398
Shaw, J. G. 1858 wb-17-425
Shaw, Samuel 1807 wb-3-144
Shaw, William 1835 wb-10-525
Shearon, Thomas W. 1854 wb-16-416
Shee, Godfort 1857 wb-17-198
Shelby, Evan 1784 wb-1-9
Shelby, John 1860 wb-18-215
Shelby, Sally 1852 wb-15-464
Shelton, Elizabeth 1843 wb-12-425*
Shelton, Elizabeth 1843 wb-12-438*
Shelton, Franklin 1840 wb-12-39*
Shelton, Godfrey 1830 wb-9-445
Shelton, Jesse 1831 wb-9-529
Shelton, Jessee 1843 wb-12-437*
Shelton, Washington G. 1833 wb-10-168
Shelton, William 1853 wb-15-572
Shelton, William H. 1834 wb-10-381
Shepherd, David Shelton 1857 wb-17-308
Shepherd, Stephen 1840 wb-12-1
Shields, Amelia 1855 wb-16-477
Shields, Thomas 1845 wb-13-319
Shields, William 1841 wb-12-168*
Shields, William C. 1855 wb-16-476
Shillcut, Thomas 1851 wb-14-670
Shinnick, Jerry 1851 wb-15-81
Shirley, Paul 1834 wb-10-327
Shivers, Abagail 1844 wb-13-82
Shivers, Noah 1833 wb-10-182
Shivers, Thomas 1829 wb-9-328
Shower, E. (Dr.) 1861 wb-18-431
Shumate, Sarah C. 1845 wb-13-271
Shumate, Willis L. 1824 wb-8-333
Shute, Asa 1815 wb-4-360
Shute, John 1844 wd-13-39
Shute, Philip 1811 wb-4-135
Shutte, Isaac 1811 wb-4-154
Simmons, Edmond 1816 wb-7-70
Simmons, Edward 1816 wb-7-13
Simmons, Edward 1847 wb-14-165
Simmons, Ezekiel 1847 wb-14-165
Simmons, James 1840 wb-12-78*
Simmons, John 1815 wb-4-362
Simmons, William 1838 wb-11-382

Simpkins, Nancy 1860 wb-18-346
Simpkins, Orman A. 1857 wb-17-260
Simpkins, Thomas 1846 wb-13-375
Simpkins, Thomas 1858 wb-17-510
Simpkins, Thomas C. 1858 wb-17-545
Simpson, Andrew 1791 wb-1-181
Simpson, B. L. 1861 wb-19-20
Simpson, William 1788 wb-1-83
Simpson, William 1808 wb-4-14
Sims, Walter 1820 wb-7-381
Singletary, Catherine 1817 wb-7-207
Singletary, John S. 1803 wb-2-318
Sisk, Martin 1823 wb-8-269
Sitler, James W. 1833 wb-10-71
Sittler, Isaac 1838 wb-11-242
Skelly, John 1834 wb-10-347
Slater, John Toms 1832 wb-9-574
Slaughter, Robert 1806 wb-3-116
Slaven, Michael C. 1856 wb-17-139
Slayden, Nicholas B. 1855 wb-16-593
Sledge, Washington A. 1843 wb-12-446*
Sloan, Frederick 1854 wb-16-278
Smiley, David sr. 1860 wb-18-404
Smiley, Emaline 1861 wb-18-449
Smiley, Robert 1823 wb-8-272
Smiley, Tresea 1842 wb-12-378*
Smith, A. 1846 wb-13-382
Smith, Abraham 1853 wb-15-477
Smith, Albert 1847 wb-14-35
Smith, Drury 1810 wb-4-110
Smith, Ezekiel 1822 wb-8-160
Smith, F. 1848 wb-14-242
Smith, George 1841 wb-12-167*
Smith, George S. 1842 wb-12-269*
Smith, James 1855 wb-16-528
Smith, James H. 1845 wb-13-322
Smith, Jesse 1822 wb-8-75
Smith, John H. 1834 wb-10-390
Smith, Joseph 1838 wb-11-217
Smith, Martin S. 1847 wb-14-90
Smith, Mary G. 1850 wb-14-524
Smith, Pleasant 1851 wb-15-32
Smith, R. P. 1853 wb-15-487
Smith, Richard 1858 wb-17-562
Smith, Robert 1832 wb-9-581
Smith, Saml. 1800 wb-2-166
Smith, Saml. 1800 wb-2-167
Smith, Samuel G. 1836 wb-10-540
Smith, Thomas 1818 wb-7-283
Smith, Thomas 1856 wb-17-70
Smith, William 1856 wb-16-616
Smith, William Sharp 1820 wb-7-373
Snary, John 1829 wb-9-319
Snow, Anthony J. 1853 wb-16-166
Snow, David C. 1833 wb-10-242

Snyder, Charles 1808 wb-3-222
Sommerville, George W. 1824 wb-8-330
Sommerville, John 1846 wb-13-474
Southall, Joseph J. B. 1853 wb-16-194
Southgate, Gertrude Vanleer 1860 wb-18-360
Spain, Stephen 1820 wb-7-454
Speece, James N. 1835 wb-10-424
Spence, David 1817 wb-7-206
Spence, James 1844 wb-13-129
Spence, John 1825 wb-8-410
Spence, John 1845 wb-13-157
Spence, Joseph 1840 wb-12-10
Spence, Joseph 1841 wb-12-18
Spence, Sarah L. 1845 wb-13-158
Spencer, David 1816 wb-4-438
Spotswood, Julia A. 1860 wb-18-361
Stan, George W. 1853 wb-16-136
Stanfield, Goodlow 1838 wb-11-487
Stark, John C. 1841 wb-12-14
Starkey, Benjamin 1860 wb-18-381
Starkey, Rebecca 1854 wb-16-263
Starr, George H. 1857 wb-17-381
Steane, John 1831 wb-9-486
Steane, Michael 1829 wb-9-352
Steele, Andrew 1858 wb-17-439
Steele, Thomas J. 1860 wb-18-319
Stegar, William 1847 wb-14-104
Stein, Joseph 1859 wb-17-601
Stenate, Geo. 1802 wb-2-266
Stephens, James 1803 wb-2-312
Stephens, John 1803 wb-2-339
Stephens, Moses 1851 wb-15-51
Stephens, Rebecca 1860 wb-18-169
Stephens, Simion 1847 wb-14-161
Stephens, Simon 1847 wb-14-137
Stephenson, George 1849 wb-14-440
Stephenson, Joshua M. 1857 wb-17-394
Stevens, Abednego 1841 wb-12-150*
Stevens, George W. 1838 wb-11-322
Stevens, Moses 1841 wb-12-148*
Stevenson, E. D. 1851 wb-14-647
Steward, William 1793 wb-1-284
Stewart, Andrew 1841 wb-12-33
Stewart, James 1834 wb-10-272
Stewart, Peter 1851 wb-15-57
Stewart, William 1837 wb-11-81
Stewart, William 1845 wb-13-147
Stewart, William 1851 wb-15-12
Still, John 1851 wb-15-120
Still, Rhodam 1850 wb-14-554
Stinnet, George 1809 wb-4-32
Stobaugh, Henry 1811 wb-4-143
Stockell, William 1847 wb-14-119
Stockwell, William 1847 wb-14-6
Stocton, Sarah 1838 wb-11-272

Stogner, Sarah 1835 wb-10-513
Stoneman, John 1802 wb-2-264
Stout, Ira 1818 wb-7-237
Stout, S. V. D. 1851 wb-15-75
Strange, Edmund G. 1855 wb-16-583
Strange, Sarah 1844 wb-13-122
Strange, Willis 1833 wb-10-157
Strawn, John 1824 wb-8-386
Stringfellow, Richard 1827 wb-9-111
Stringfellow, Robert 1815 wb-4-364
Stringfellow, William 1847 wb-14-65
Stron, John 1825 wb-8-412
Strong, John 1816 wb-4-439
Strong, John 1816 wb-7-53
Strother, George 1816 wb-7-24
Strother, John 1816 wb-4-431
Strother, John 1816 wb-7-20
Stuart, Margaret 1808 wb-4-7
Stuart, William 1808 wb-3-191
Stuart, William 1812 wb-4-196
Stuart, Wm. 1794 wb-1-304
Stubblefield, Clement 1845 wb-13-191
Stull, George 1854 wb-16-361
Stull, Nancy (Mrs.) 1852 wb-15-212
Stull, Rachiel 1847 wb-14-111
Stull, Zacheriah 1819 wb-7-314
Stump, Albert G. 1836 wb-10-601
Stump, Albert G. 1853 wb-15-568
Stump, F. H. 1848 wb-14-243
Stump, Frederick 1820 wb-7-501
Stump, John 1854 wb-16-418
Stump, Jonathan 1806 wb-3-77
Stump, Nancy B. 1857 wb-17-298
Stump, Rachel 1860 wb-18-238
Stump, Rebecca W. 1853 wb-16-165
Sturdevant, Henry W. 1826 wb-9-36
Sturdivant, Josiah M. 1830 wb-9-446
Sugg, Aquila 1789 wb-1-97
Suggs, Noah 1798 wb-2-119
Sullivan, W. W. 1850 wb-14-646
Sullivan, W. W. 1851 wb-14-618
Sullivan, William 1808 wb-3-186
Sumner, Duke William 1844 wb-13-103
Sumner, Exum P. 1852 wb-15-271
Sumner, Jacob B. 1815 wb-4-343
Sumner, Mary 1849 wb-14-612
Sures, Charles 1809 wb-4-47
Sutton, Malichiah 1794 wb-2-3
Sutton, Stephen 1838 wb-11-218
Swann, Jane C. 1834 wb-10-379
Swann, William 1854 wb-16-213
Swann, Willis 1832 wb-9-597
Swearingen, Mary E. 1861 wb-18-581
Sweeny, B. F. 1861 wb-18-467
Swenson, James M. 1857 wb-17-217

Swenson, John M. 1854 wb-16-275
Swift, John 1808 wb-3-218
Swingston, Rachel 1845 wb-13-275
Tabb, James A. 1804 wb-2-384
Tait, Margaret 1816 wb-4-462
Tait, Robert 1804 wb-2-380
Tait, William 1816 wb-4-458
Tait, William 1816 wb-7-42
Talbert, Thomas 1847 wb-14-23
Talbot, Eli 1833 wb-10-229
Talbot, Jane 1809 wb-4-78
Talbot, Mathew 1804 wb-2-394
Talbot, Mathew 1815 wb-4-333
Talbot, Thomas 1833 wb-10-184
Talbott, Mathew 1805 wb-3-8
Talley, David 1853 wb-15-571
Talley, Nelson 1853 wb-16-70
Tally, Reuben 1852 wb-15-347
Tankesley, Francis 1847 wb-14-91
Tanksley, Louisa J. 1852 wb-15-424
Tarkinton, Zabulon 1799 wb-2-141
Tarver, Jane W. 1857 wb-17-256
Tate, John 1826 wb-9-31
Tate, Rebecca 1835 wb-10-494
Tatum, Howell 1823 wb-8-219
Tatum, James 1821 wb-8-28
Tatum, Nathaniel 1844 wb-13-78
Taylor, Berry 1830 wb-9-379
Taylor, Chesley 1840 wb-12-88*
Taylor, Green B. 1832 wb-9-617
Taylor, Henry 1811 wb-4-158
Taylor, Henry 1830 wb-9-454
Taylor, Isaac 1840 wb-12-79*
Taylor, J. M. 1856 wb-17-56
Taylor, James M. 1857 wb-17-370
Taylor, Joel R. 1838 wb-11-174
Taylor, John 1836 wb-10-538
Taylor, Jos. R. 1837 wb-11-5
Taylor, Joseph 1851 wb-14-622
Taylor, Josiah 1852 wb-15-464
Taylor, Rachel 1859 wb-18-48
Taylor, Robert 1847 wb-14-133
Taylor, Thomas 1815 wb-4-393
Taylor, Thomas 1827 wb-9-90
Taylor, Thomas 1853 wb-16-59
Telford, Sarah 1852 wb-15-244
Temple, Leston 1819 wb-7-354
Tennain?, Lemuel 1837 wb-11-62
Tennison, Joseph 1861 wb-19-32
Tenny, E. H. 1861 wb-18-472
Terrell, William 1804 wb-2-396
Terry, Burrell 1852 wb-15-300
Terry, Jeremiah 1851 wb-15-55
Thomas, Abijah 1814 wb-4-321
Thomas, Elisha 1860 wb-18-235

Thomas, George G. (Dr.) 1808 wb-4-5
Thomas, Jesse W. 1816 wb-4-470
Thomas, Jesse W. 1816 wb-7-107
Thomas, Jno. 1803 wb-2-335
Thomas, John 1803 wb-2-334
Thomas, John 1804 wb-2-347
Thomas, John 1816 wb-7-97
Thomas, John 1833 wb-10-161
Thomas, John 1844 wb-13-115
Thomas, John 1858 wb-17-422
Thomas, Joshua 1795 wb-2-13
Thomas, Micah 1857 wb-17-379
Thomas, Philip 1835 wb-10-521
Thomas, Robert 1838 wb-11-453
Thomas, William 1798 wb-2-111
Thomas, William 1847 wb-14-163
Thompson*, Neal 1814 wb-4-296
Thompson, Alfred 1843 wb-13-1
Thompson, Allen 1852 wb-15-438
Thompson, Allen 1852 wb-15-455
Thompson, Almeda 1853 wb-15-577
Thompson, Elizabeth 1855 wb-16-532
Thompson, Ephraim 1834 wb-10-385
Thompson, Frederick 1815 wb-4-361
Thompson, Horace D. 1860 wb-18-242
Thompson, James 1792 wb-1-260
Thompson, Jason 1833 wb-10-258
Thompson, John 1793 wb-1-290
Thompson, John W. 1855 wb-16-564
Thompson, Polly D. 1859 wb-17-605
Thompson, Robert 1821 wb-7-499
Thompson, Saml. 1803 wb-2-338
Thompson, William P. 1840 wb-12-95*
Thompson, William sr. 1837 wb-11-67
Thornton, George L. 1851 wb-15-2
Thornton, Reuben S. 1826 wb-9-56
Thorpe, John 1852 wb-15-327
Thorpe, John 1852 wb-15-395
Tilford, Elizabeth 1835 wb-10-517
Tilford, W. H. 1851 wb-14-629
Timms, Elizabeth 1861 wb-18-445
Timms, Jabez 1857 wb-17-161
Tindall, John 1854 wb-16-220
Tindall, John 1855 wb-16-511
Tinnen, Lemuel 1835 wb-10-412
Tipton, Edward 1814 wb-4-291
Titcomb, S. H. 1861 wb-18-533
Todd, John N. 1846 wb-13-396
Tolbert, Thomas 1850 wb-14-505
Toney, W. H. C. 1853 wb-16-100
Toope, Otto 1841 wb-12-237*
Topp, John 1837 wb-11-24
Torbitt, George W. 1852 wb-15-459
Towland, Robert 1851 wb-15-192
Towles, Oliver 1857 wb-17-335

Tramel, Nicholas 1784 wb-1-10
Tribble, Spilsby 1799 wb-2-154
Trigg, Guy S. 1809 wb-4-60
Trimble, James 1824 wb-8-368
Troost, Gerard 1851 wb-15-123
Trousdale, Elizabeth 1853 wb-16-89
Tucker, Anderson 1857 wb-17-293
Tucker, Edmond 1836 wb-10-556
Tucker, John Edmond 1839 wb-11-596
Tucker, Randal 1852 wb-15-268
Turbeville, Jefferson 1848 wd-14-225
Turbeville, Rutha 1817 wb-7-128
Turbeville, Wilie 1848 wb-14-243
Turbeville, Wilkins S. 1842 wb-12-310*
Turley, James 1840 wb-12-32
Turley, Jennett 1838 wb-11-421
Turner, George 1805 wb-3-37
Turner, James 1811 wb-4-158
Turner, James 1825 wb-8-439
Turner, Jno. 1784? wb-1-25
Turner, Joseph B. 1819 wb-7-315
Turner, Lemuel T. 1816 wb-4-425
Turner, Lemuel T. 1816 wb-7-18
Turner, Martha 1839 wb-11-578
Turner, Medicus R. 1832 wb-9-618
Turner, R. A. 1852 wb-15-236
Turner, Richard A. 1852 wb-15-219
Turner, Thomas 1832 wb-9-586
Turner, W. W. 1854 wb-16-358
Tyner, William C. 1851 wb-14-621
Tyree, Henry 1852 wb-15-348
Underwood, Alexr. 1800 wb-2-192
Underwood, Catharine 1858 wb-17-476
Utley, William H. 1818 wb-7-240
Vance, Elisha Q. 1855 wb-16-577
Vanderville, John 1845 wb-13-357
Vanleer, Bernard 1833 wb-10-65
Vanleer, Hannah 1836 wb-10-544
Vaughan, Randolph 1858 wb-17-457
Vaughn, David 1838 wb-11-182
Vaughn, J. C. 1848 wb-14-283
Vaughn, Martha 1835 wb-10-515
Vaughn, Sarah 1857 wb-17-338
Vaulx, Catherine 1852 wb-15-361
Vaulx, Daniel 1815 wb-4-389
Vaulx, Daniel 1816 wb-7-52
Vernon, Saml. 1786 wb-1-46
Vick, Robert 1826 wb-9-1
Vincent, Julia 1859 wb-17-622
Wade, Francis 1844 wb-13-60
Waggoner, Matthew 1854 wb-16-349
Wagler, John 1814 wb-4-305
Wagner, Charles Henry 1857 wb-17-262
Wagoner, Jacob 1858 wb-17-510
Walch, John B. 1838 wb-11-468

Walden, Jno. W. 1860 wb-18-382
Waldron, J. W. 1861 wb-18-476
Waldron, Sarah D. 1834 wb-10-287
Waldron, William 1857 wb-17-382
Walker, Alexander 1840 wb-12-33
Walker, Elmore 1834 wb-10-348
Walker, James 1830 wb-9-377
Walker, Jennet 1806 wb-3-98
Walker, Jennit 1806 wb-3-99
Walker, John 1818 wb-7-247
Walker, John A. 1861 wb-18-625
Walker, Jonathan 1816 wb-7-10
Walker, Joseph W. 1861 wb-18-535
Walker, Margaret 1841 wb-12-177*
Walker, Mathew P. 1851 wb-14-573
Walker, Nancy 1836 wb-10-582
Walker, Nicholas 1835 wb-10-519
Walker, Philip 1802 wb-2-231
Walker, Philip 1826 wb-9-66
Walker, Pleasant H. 1833 wb-10-159
Walker, Pleasant H. 1833 wb-10-72
Walker, Robert T. 1838 wb-11-219
Walker, William 1815 wb-4-339
Wallace, B. R. B. 1851 wb-14-582
Wallace, Jesse 1825 wb-8-463
Wallace, William 1825 wb-8-445
Waller, Joel 1842 wb-12-302*
Waller, Thomas 1846 wb-13-373
Walton, William J. 1859 wb-18-106
Wand, James 1845 wb-13-230
Ward, Daniel 1861 wb-18-468
Ward, Nancy 1831 wb-9-564
Ward, Rebecah 1808 wb-3-214
Ward, Sarah 1853 wb-15-530
Ward, William C. 1828 wb-9-170
Warmack, Richard 1861 wb-18-420
Warmack, Thomas 1841 wb-12-219*
Warmack, William 1840 wb-12-39*
Warmouth, John 1852 wb-15-325
Warmuth, Thomas 1853 wb-16-129
Warmuth, William 1860 wb-18-380
Warren, Thomas 1810 wb-4-92
Washington, Gilbert J. 1847 wb-14-51
Washington, Gray 1808 wb-4-18
Washington, James G. 1838 wb-11-397
Washington, James G. 1852 wb-15-286
Washington, Janet 1828 wb-9-155
Wates, Alexander 1851 wb-15-140
Watkins, Isaac 1833 wb-10-196
Watkins, Jacob 1799 wb-2-160
Watkins, Phillip 1852 wb-15-326
Watkins, Thomas 1828 wb-9-269
Watkins, Thomas J. 1838 wb-11-459
Watkins, Thomas J. 1839 wb-11-522
Watkins, Thomas S. 1841 wb-12-113*

Watkins, William 1841 wb-12-122*
Watkins, William E. 1851 wb-15-152
Watkins, William E. jr. 1848 wb-14-282
Watson, David R. 1851 wb-15-122
Watson, James 1845 wb-13-320
Watson, Jonathan R. 1858 wb-17-494
Watson, Josiah 1833 wb-10-90
Watson, Susan 1845 wb-13-294
Watson, W. D. 1856 wb-17-70
Weakley, Nimrod 1814 wb-4-290
Weakley, Robert 1845 wb-13-267
Weakley, Robert 1859 wb-17-584
Weakley, Samuel 1832 wb-10-39
Weatherford, Nancy 1831 wb-9-540
Weatherly, William 1846 wb-13-384
Webb, John 1842 wb-12-327*
Webb, John 1859 wb-17-626
Webber, John 1853 wb-15-518
Welch, Thomas 1833 wb-10-208
Welch, Thomas 1833 wb-10-227
Wells, Hiram 1837 wb-11-124
Wells, William 1823 wb-8-184
Wendel, William 1844 wd-13-23
Wesling, H. H. 1856 wb-17-102
Wessells, John 1860 wb-18-250
West, Mary Ann 1847 wb-14-101
West, Micajah 1805 wb-3-34
West, Micajah 1805 wb-3-48
Westmoreland, Jessee 1811 wb-4-160
Westmoreland, Reuben 1818 wb-7-274
Wetherald, James 1828 wb-9-245
Wetzel, Lewis 1848 wb-14-267
Wharton, C. J. 1857 wb-17-251
Wharton, C. J. F. 1856 wb-17-271
Wharton, George 1824 wb-8-383
Wharton, Jesse 1833 wb-10-181
Wharton, John 1816 wb-4-467
Wharton, Lucinda 1849 wb-14-421
Wharton, Samuel L. 1833 wb-10-172
Wharton, William 1816 wb-7-31
Wheaton, Daniel 1805 wb-3-16
Wheless, Wesley 1861 wb-18-637
Whitaker, Robert W. 1852 wb-15-443
White, Arthur 1820 wb-7-422
White, Beverly W. 1839 wb-11-575
White, J. N. 1848 wd-14-186
White, Jesse N. 1851 wb-14-591
White, Joseph 1852 wb-15-375
White, Joshua 1815 wb-4-354
White, Joshua 1820 wb-7-423
White, Lucy 1816 wb-7-74
White, R. J. 1855 wb-16-455
White, Robert J. 1858 wb-17-436
White, Sarah 1820 wb-7-416
White, Thomas B. 1855 wb-16-530

White, William 1837 wb-11-27
White, Willis 1832 wb-10-9
Whiteside, Thomas 1832 wb-9-571
Whitfield, John W. 1848 wb-14-273
Whiting, John 1834 wb-10-286
Whitley, Joab 1816 wb-4-428
Whitley, Thomas 1845 wb-13-233
Whitsctt, Jane 1842 wb-12-385*
Whitsett, Reuben E. 1853 wb-16-188
Whitsett, Ruben 1853 wb-16-111
Whitsitt, James 1850 wb-14-509
Whitsitt, James M. 1840 wb-12-84*
Whitsitt, Joseph W. 1860 wb-18-356
Whittemore, Abraham 1842 wb-12-270*
Whittemore, Clement 1826 wb-8-552
Whittemore, Clemment 1826 wb-9-18
Whittemore, John H. 1861 wb-18-455
Whittemore, Nancy 1828 wb-9-268
Whittemore, William V. 1861 wb-18-457
Whyte, Phereby S. 1855 wb-16-591
Whyte, Robert 1845 wb-13-216
Wiggins, Henry 1798 wb-2-108
Wigglesworth, Benjamin 1853 wb-16-134
Wilcox, Thomas 1814 wb-4-290
Wilcox, Thomas 1834 wb-10-375
Wilkerson, William 1843 wb-12-427*
Wilkes, James 1830 wb-9-367
Wilkes, Thomas 1810 wb-4-107
Wilkins, Benjamin 1845 wb-13-248
Wilkinson, Benjamin 1820 wb-7-409
Wilkinson, Jesse B. 1819 wb-7-314
Wilkinson, Jonathan 1858 wb-17-440
Wilkinson, Kinchen T. 1817 wb-7-163
Wilkinson, Mournen 1844 wd-13-25
Wilkinson, William 1841 wb-12-102*
Wilkinson, William sr. 1829 wb-9-274
Wilkison, Jessee 1799 wb-2-185
Wilks, Mary 1838 wb-11-335
Williams, Archelaus 1812 wb-4-188
Williams, C. 1836 wb-10-643
Williams, Christopher 1838 wb-11-194
Williams, Curtis 1789 wb-1-123
Williams, Daniel Sr. 1794 wb-1-302
Williams, Etheldred 1849 wb-14-288
Williams, Evander M. 1857 wb-17-179
Williams, Francis 1808 wb-3-195
Williams, Isaac 1852 wb-15-260
Williams, James 1847 wb-14-24
Williams, James R. 1847 wb-14-36
Williams, Jane 1811 wb-4-164
Williams, John 1805 wb-3-15
Williams, John 1809 wb-4-29
Williams, John 1819 wb-7-335
Williams, John sr. 1859 wb-17-612
Williams, Jonathan 1819 wb-7-331

Williams, Josiah F. 1852 wb-15-374
Williams, Leoner 1850 wb-14-476
Williams, Littleberry 1818 wb-7-229
Williams, Margaret 1859 wb-18-106
Williams, Martha 1857 wb-17-377
Williams, Mathew 1820 wb-7-413
Williams, Nathan 1844 wb-13-73
Williams, Nimrod 1819 wb-7-323
Williams, Philimon 1796 wb-2-44
Williams, Philip 1842 wb-12-385*
Williams, R. N. 1857 wb-17-357
Williams, Robert 1826 wb-9-67
Williams, Simon 1852 wb-15-427
Williams, Thomas 1816 wb-7-5
Williams, Thomas S. 1851 wb-14-579
Williams, Tully 1820 wb-7-412
Williams, William 1824 wb-8-307
Williams, Willis 1837 wb-11-77
Williams, Wilson 1858 wb-17-489
Williams, Wilson 1858 wb-17-536
Williamson, James 1857 wb-17-189
Williamson, Jas. 1802 wb-2-256
Williamson, John 1834 wb-10-289
Wills, David 1822 wb-8-126
Willson, Aaron 1808 wb-4-18
Wilson, Elizabeth 1859 wb-18-65
Wilson, George 1850 wb-14-481
Wilson, James 1811 wb-4-143
Wilson, James 1811 wb-4-154
Wilson, John 1821 wb-7-494
Wilson, John R. 1854 wb-16-429
Wilson, Robert 1860 wb-18-234
Wilson, Thomas 1811 wb-4-162
Wilson, Thomas 1812 wb-4-174
Wilson, Thomas 1853 wb-16-185
Wilson, William C. 1841 wb-12-129*
Wilson, William F. 1859 wb-17-622
Windle, Susannah 1816 wb-4-465
Winfield, John G. 1838 wb-11-473
Winfrey, John S. 1838 wb-11-190
Winn, Richard 1809 wb-4-46
Winn, Richard 1816 wb-7-16
Winston, Peter M. 1847 wb-14-8
Winter, Robert 1853 wb-15-478
Wisner, Martin 1802 wb-2-224
Witt, Mills 1833 wb-10-161
Woehrle, Jacob C. 1853 wb-16-87
Woehrle, J. C. 1852 wb-15-222
Wolf, Elizabeth 1857 wb-17-258
Wolf, Phillip P. 1837 wb-11-1
Wolfe, Samuel 1848 wb-14-242
Wood, John L. 1813 wb-4-210
Wood, John Scott 1812 wb-4-181
Wood, Margaret 1815 wb-4-363
Wood, Margaret 1815 wb-4-376

Wood, Robert 1843 wb-12-399*
Woodard, Daniel 1820 wb-7-409
Woodard, Thomas 1809 wb-4-32
Woodcock, John 1834 wb-10-306
Woodcock, Margaret 1861 wb-19-1
Woodfin, William 1812 wb-4-193
Woods, David 1854 wb-16-311
Woods, Joseph 1860 wb-18-168
Woodson, Thomas J. 1836 wb-10-537
Woodward, Caroline M. 1841 wb-12-134*
Woodward, Edmond 1851 wb-15-146
Woodward, Edward 1848 wb-14-258
Woodward, George P. 1851 wb-14-587
Woodward, John 1853 wb-16-181
Woodward, Judith 1853 wb-16-174
Woodward, Micajah 1808 wb-4-6
Woodward, Thos. 1809 wb-4-48
Work, Martha 1855 wb-16-510
Work, Samuel 1851 wb-14-574
Wray, William 1843 wb-12-465*
Wray, William 1853 wb-16-123
Wright, Charles 1826 wb-9-61
Wright, Charles 1846 wb-13-367
Wright, Francis 1824 wb-8-385
Wright, Hollis 1851 wb-15-36
Wright, Hollis 1851 wb-15-8
Wright, James 1816 wb-7-101
Wright, James 1829 wb-9-344
Wright, John 1851 wb-15-60
Wright, John 1858 wb-17-563
Wright, John B. 1836 wb-10-641
Wright, John M. 1856 wb-17-84
Wright, Joseph 1831 wb-9-503
Wright, Polley 1854 wb-16-315
Wright, William 1815 wb-4-339
Wyatt, Spencer 1853 wb-15-574
Wynne, Albert H. 1851 wb-14-563
Yarbrough, James 1861 wb-18-606
Yeatman, Thomas 1834 wb-10-277
Yellowby, William G. 1840 wb-12-77*
Young, Daniel 1820 wb-7-421
Young, Daniel 1860 wb-18-231
Young, Daniel 1860 wb-18-232
Young, Elenor 1826 wb-8-535
Young, F. J. 1842 wb-12-325*
Young, Harriet 1838 wb-11-112
Young, John S. 1860 wb-18-347
Young, Mark 1861 wb-18-446
Young, Mark sr. 1859 wb-17-616
Young, Mary 1857 wb-17-306
Zachary, Crawford 1836 wb-10-597
Zachary, G. G. 1852 wb-15-270
Zachary, Griffin G. 1853 wb-16-122
Zollicoffer, G. D. 1855 wb-16-455